Anglo-Saxon Tools

Dennis Riley

Published 2014 by
Anglo-Saxon Books
Hereward, Black Bank Business Centre
Little Downham, Ely,
Cambridgeshire CB6 2UA, England

Printed and bound by
Lightning Source
Australia, England, USA

PL

Contents © Dennis Riley
Design/layout © Anglo-Saxon Books

All rights reserved. No part of this publication may be reproduced or transmitted in any form or by any means, electronic or mechanical including photo-copying, recording or any information storage or retrieval system, without prior permission in writing from the publisher, except for the quotation of brief passages in connection with a review written for inclusion in a magazine or newspaper.

This book may not be lent, resold, hired out or otherwise disposed of by way of trade in any form of binding or cover other than that in which it is published, without the prior consent of the publishers.

ISBN 9781898281726

To My Father's Father
Clifford
Son of Harold
Son of Alfred
Son of William
Back unto the beginning

Contents

- Contents 4
- Acknowledgments 8
- Glossary 8
- Introduction 9
- 1 The Physical Evidence 11
  - Deposition 11
  - Creation 12
  - Survival of the Wettest 12
  - Evidence of Tooling 13
  - Longevity of Tool-Types - The Nazeing Hoard 13
  - The Grave Evidence 14
    - Tools versus Dress Artefacts 15
- 2 The Anglo-Saxon Smith 17
  - Status 17
  - Left-Handed Craftsmen 19
  - Evidence for Left- and Right-Handedness 19
  - Dead Man's Tools 20
  - Anglo-Saxon Burial practice 20
  - Interpretation of Cemetery Finds: The Acquisition and Use of Artefacts 21
  - The Smith's Grave at Tattershall Thorpe 23
- 3 Tool Types in Anglo-Saxon Contexts 29
  - Shears 29
  - Tradition 31
  - General Utility 31
  - Ambidexterity 31
  - Accident of Manufacture 31
  - Post Migration Cultural Change 31
    - Snips and Cutters 32
- 4 Tool Finds by Occupation 33
  - Hones 33
  - Knives 38
    - Serrated Knives 40
    - Folding Knives 40
    - Pivoting Knives 41
  - Metalworking Tools 42
    - Hammers 42

Contents

- Anvils 44
- Tongs 46
- Snips & Cutters 48
- Files 49
- Chisels 51
- Punches 54
- Tanged Punches 56
- Nail Irons and Draw-Plates 57
- Pritchels 58
- Blacksmiths' Clips 59
- Soldering Boats 60
- Reamers 61

Woodworking Tools 62
- Axes 62
  - Type 1 63
  - Type 2 63
  - Types 3, 4 and 5 65
- Adzes 66
- Spoon Augers 68
- Breast Augers 70
- Chisels and Gouges 70
- Shaves 71
  - Curved or Bowl Shaves 72
  - Draw Knives 72
  - Spoke Shaves 74
- Hammers and Mallets 76
- Bow Drills 77
- Gimlets & Borers 78
- Wedges 78
- Lathes 80
- Planes 82

Leatherworking Tools 83
- Slickers 83
- Lunettes 84
- Shears 85
- Creasers 86
- Tanning Tool 86
- Shoe Lasts 86
- Smaller Hand Tools – Gouges, Pegs, Awls 87

Contents

Bone- and Antler-Working Tools 88
- Saws 89
- Rasps 91
- Awls 91
- Rivetted Mounts 92
- Clamps 93

Textile-Workers' Tools 94
- Primary Wool Processing Tools 95
  - Shears 95
  - Wool Cards 98
- Primary Plant Fibre Processing Tools 100
  - Ripplers 100
  - Pounders 101
  - Scutching Knives 101
  - Heckles 102
- Fabric Processing Tools 102
  - Spinning Tools 103
  - Weaving Tools 106
  - Needles 109
- Tablet Weaving 112

Agricultural Tools 112
- Land Clearance Tools 113
  - Bills and Billhooks 113
  - Fauchards 113
- Ploughing Tools 114
  - Ploughshares 115
  - Coulters 115
  - Mattocks 116
- Drainage and Ditching Tools 117
  - Picks 117
  - Shovels 118
  - Spades 120
- Harvesting Tools 121
  - Scythes 121
  - Sickles and Reaping Hooks 121
  - Pitchforks 123
- Miscellaneous Tools 123
  - Sharpening Steels 123
  - Bread Peels 125

Contents

    Flesh Hooks and Forks 125
    Dry Rakes 126
    Mill Picks 126
  Fishing Tackle 127
    Fish Spear 127
    Fish Hooks 127
    Net Weights 129
  Pottery stamps 129
5 Tool Signatures 131
6 The Portable Antiquities Scheme 133
7 Conclusion 135
Appendix 1 Stamp Forms in Non-Ferrous Metal 136
Appendix 2 Anglo-Saxon Tool Ferrules 145
Appendix 3 Anglo-Saxon Tools Wordlist 147
Bibliography 149

Acknowledgments

No man is an island, especially when he writes a book so I would like to mark out for special thanks Stephen Pollington, for putting up with my late night emails on tedious points and his encouraging noises as my book progressed. Likewise Dr. Kevin Leahy for offering as much information as I requested of him - and more - and also listing here the Scraptoft hoard in advance of its official publication.

I hope this little tome does not dishonour them!

Dennis Riley, 2013

Glossary

coulter	A piece of the plough which cuts through the soil
fauchard	A type of billhook with an extension to the rear of the blade
hone	A stone for putting the final sharp edge on a blade
lunette	A leatherworking knife with a crescentic blade
naalbinding	A single-needle knitting technique similar to crochet
mattock	A wooden mallet for breaking up clods of earth
pritchel	A kind of punch for use on hot metal
reamer	A tool for enlarging a punched hole
rippler	A flax-working comb
slicker	A flat-bladed leatherworking knife
ccutching knife	A flat flax-working tool
unidexter	A person favouring one hand over the other
whetstone	A tool for sharpening a blade

Introduction

This book has the title 'Anglo-Saxon Tools' but it would be more accurate to described it as 'tools used by the Anglo-Saxons'. The reason is that the tools and utensils they employed in their daily lives were much the same as those used at that time in Scandinavia and elsewhere in Europe, which was due to a mixture of shared heritage and trade. The Anglo-Saxons did not invent any new tools and the technology available to them was not more advanced than that used by their European neighbours. The tools had been in widespread use for centuries - in some cases even millennia - prior to the Anglo-Saxon period in Britain.

The incidence of tool use can be traced back through the Roman period, the Iron Age, the Bronze Age and, in some transmuted form, further back into the Neolithic period (New Stone Age). In modern times, we regard tools as being mostly made from widely available iron and steel but in the period under discussion toolmakers regularly employed wood, bone, antler, stone and pottery in their construction. All these tools would have been constructed from locally available materials wherever possible, to suit local requirements.

References are made in this book to Continental and Scandinavian finds and styles where a common ancestry or tool type exists. It should be noted that although there are only a few variations in tool construction it is nonetheless possible to infer developing themes which may indicate 'tribal' styles. However, the effects of trade and mutation through imperfect duplication make any definitive analysis difficult, if not impossible.

Tools should not be seen as mere artefacts but as a means for expressing a communal identity and building a more advanced and sophisticated society.

Tools are sometimes found as grave goods so it seems prudent to explore their social context - at least their presence in or absence from the burial rite. On the whole, tools are disparate finds confined to tool hoards, casual losses and (rarely) grave-goods with inhumations - which has made the task of writing this book quite complex. The method employed here is to investigate tools on the basis of purpose or activity rather than by find-spot or hoard, so giving the reader a broad spectrum of information regarding tool form, function and use. The arms, armour and social structure of Anglo-Saxon England is well understood and has received much research; it is hoped that this book will contribute to the understanding of some of the more routine aspects of the Anglo-Saxon way-of-life.

Illustrations in this book show reconstructions of the excavated tools rather than line drawings or photos of the original carefully shaped pieces of rust. To this end the tools shown fall into two categories: (i) those that are accurate reproductions of the tools in question and (ii) those that can be called "generic reconstructions" in which the general style of the tool is captured. The reconstructions show the tools as they may have originally looked and as a consequence the reconstructions can be used as the original tools would have been. This gives us a further insight into the ability of the tool to do its job and the amount of work it was capable of.

In each discussion a section on reconstructive tool use has been included which elevates the artefact from a dry and dusty museum exhibit into a functional living thing thereby allowing the user to experience the problems and pleasures that the Anglo-Saxons encountered.

Figure 1 Reproduction tool set - the Bygland smith's grave assemblage

1 The Physical Evidence

Deposition

As with most created items, tools are made, tools are used and tools are eventually lost, broken or buried: all these processes are partly random. Two axes could be manufactured by the smith on the same day; the first may see two hundred years of use and the second axe becomes lost by the end of the first day of its birth! Each tool-find therefore provides an imperfect view of the world it came from. Seriation of finds is effectively impossible as most tool forms have changed little from the Roman period (and in some cases even earlier) up to the Industrial Revolution in the British Isles.[1] Since such little evidence for tools is found in graves, we cannot use the context of grave goods to help us here.

The 'heirloom factor' also contributes to the lack of datable finds as Theune comments:[2]

> *"The heirloom factor undermines all attempts at dating by association"*

The heirloom factor is usually associated with valued grave goods - the treasured ring of an uncle, the bracelet of a grandmother, etc. - where the deposition date may be some decades later than the date of manufacture. With tools, however, a different type of heirloom factor seems evident in that the lack of tool burials associated with inhumations suggests the heirlooms continue to exist above ground in the realm of the living. This would appear to be a defined and intentional act on the part of the family of the deceased and is likely to reflect social need rather than an aspect of funerary practice, aspects of which we will investigate later (p.14).

Tool hoards supply us with an interesting array of tools for investigation. The motive behind the burial of hoards is not always discernible but the most likely reason is to hide them from view either as the proceeds of theft or an attempt to avoid it. The Mästermyr hoard (Gotland, circa 1000AD)[3] is an interesting and rare case where the tool chest was an unfortunate loss, presumably during transport. The types of tool in the chest suggest that more than one chest was being transported but only one lost. Casual loss in buildings and manufacturing centres provides us with much valuable information, not only about the tools but also the circumstance of their use and the type of community they came from. Notable among these finds are the large collections from Flixborough (Lincolnshire)[4] and Coppergate (York)[5] and the smaller groups of finds from Carlton Coleville (Suffolk)[6] and other sites. Collectively they provide a picture of the technology of the Anglo-Saxon period and a snapshot of daily life in a variety of communities.

---

[1] Hinton, 2000; Coatsworth & Pinder, 2002; Leahy, 2003, pp.117-23
[2] Theune, 1999. pp34
[3] Arwidsson & Berg, 1983
[4] Evans & Loveluck, 2009
[5] Ottaway, 1992, 17/6
[6] Lucy, Tipper & Dickens, 2009

Creation

All tools are brought into being by the mind and hand that create them. In most instances it is the smith with his work in iron and steel, as Pollington[7] remarks:

> *"In many cultures, the smith's position is figuratively similar to that of the midwife - he oversees the coming-into-being of a new entity"*

This statement is true of any artisan who creates a tool, utensil or item for use, but the smith is at the pinnacle of the technological ladder in the Anglo-Saxon period and we are fortunate that a wide selection of the smith's products survive for investigation (though his tools are unfortunately rare finds).

Other skilled craftsman, such as wood workers and stone workers, used implements made by a smith, and they could produce tools of their own from wood, pottery, stone and other materials[8] but none used such advanced technology as the smith.

We do not know directly the extent to which women were involved in tool making but it is safe to assume that in the production of fabrics they would have had some involvement in maintaining and making alterations to the tools they used. Every stratum of society would have had some experience in the making of tools for household use - from the mundane shaping of wooden pegs or the production of leather stamps in bone, antler or wood, to the crafting of pole-lathes for woodworking and the manufacture of shovels, hoes and rakes, which were essential for maintaining their fields.

Survival of the Wettest

Not all tools are made of iron and steel. As many as possible would have been constructed from other, cheaper and more readily available materials. Most people had the necessary skills to produce items from wood, bone and antler. These materials are organic in nature and are subject to decay, so after a thousand years in the ground little evidence remains of them. Countless such tools must have been lost to the processes of time: how many wooden spindle whorls and shafts have been lost from the burial record with the consequence that our presumptions are skewed towards the surviving inorganic finds? Fortunately, boggy ground often preserves these organic materials in a remarkable state due to the anaerobic conditions present. The organic (mainly wooden) finds from Anglo-Scandinavian Coppergate (York)[9] gives us a rare insight into their construction and diversity. Further afield, the work undertaken at Viking and medieval Novgorod[10] in Russia shows just what we have lost.

---

[7] Pollington, Kerr & Hammond, 2010, p.124ff
[8] Leahy, 2003
[9] Morris, 2000, AY17/13
[10] Brisbane & Hather (editors), 2007

1 The Physical Evidence

Evidence of Tooling

A further aid to the understanding of tools and their uses comes from the signatures they leave behind during the manufacture of other components: from the shape and dimensions of the grooves created in the making of bowls we can reconstruct the likely size of shaves; from the profile of bored holes we can reconstruct spoon augers; and, in the case of the cask heads from Coppergate (York),[11] we can see the evidence of iron-tipped dividers on makers' marks. So, although no direct evidence for dividers has yet been found, we know from the tool-marks that they were in use, although we cannot know what they looked like.

We also have manuscript depictions and tapestries, although such pictorial representations are always open to interpretation. Lastly we have the verbal evidence - those Anglo-Saxon words for tools that we have not yet found but know to have existed. It seems prudent to include a word list of tools (Appendix 3) for those interested in grappling with the complexities of the Old English language. So, we can make up an entire theoretical toolbox of items available and in use during the Anglo-Saxon period.

Longevity of Tool-Types - The Nazeing Hoard

The 'Nazeing hoard' (from Nazeing, Essex) was originally found in 1972 but it was not until 1980 that the material was subjected to analysis.[12] It contained 17 objects comprising 4 axes, 4 spearheads, an unsocketed gouge, a chisel, a small hammer, a ploughshare, a three-pronged fish spear (unusual in the Anglo-Saxon period), a copper-alloy ring and a copper-alloy cup; all were damaged.

The important items for dating were the four axes:

- a small Roman carpenter's axehead similar to one in Reading museum, from Silchester,[13] possibly of Romano-British origin;
- a 'Wheeler type 1' axehead, likely to be of 8th to 11th century date;
- a large 'Wheeler type IV' axehead dated to 875-950 AD;
- a smaller lightweight axehead that, at the time of discovery, had no known direct parallels in Britain.

The hoard items were all damaged and were likely to have gone for reworking. The hoard deposition date is presumed to be some time in the 11th century, indicating that some of the tools may have been in use for up to 500 years. This is entirely possible as axes can be re-worked and re steeled many times, which gives rise to the possibility of late Anglo-Saxon tools still being in use in the 13th and 14th centuries.

---

[11] Morris, 2000, AY17/13 pp.2259
[12] Morris, 1983
[13] Goodman, 1965

1 The Physical Evidence

The Grave Evidence

Tools represent a 'stepping stone' between man's ideas and their realisation, the transition from abstract to the concrete. Tools are an extension of man's mind and, as such, have given rise to a multitude of variant forms for all the tasks that can be imagined. The relationship between mind and tool is complex, with both men and women being highly dependent on their use of tools to maintain their daily life. The main thrust outlined here is the relationship between tool and user in death and beyond, and the use of tools as part of the funerary rite. In male inhumations the evidence is slight, but female inhumations tell a different story.

Figure 2 A reproduction of the Nazeing trident or fish-spear.

Our primary source comes from the inhumations. From these burials it is possible to form a number of speculative ideas as to the relationship between the interred and the contents of the grave - or more specifically the user and the tool. There are variations between both male and female finds, but from these finds, identified by period and gender, a picture emerges.

1 The Physical Evidence

Included in the inhumation evidence is the 'smith's grave' from Tattershall Thorpe (Lincolnshire).[14] It is necessary to place this exceptional burial in some sort of context as it is impossible to produce a meaningful analysis of day-to-day tool deposition on the basis of one spectacular find. In the case of the Tattershall Thorpe find, the particular factor is that it is the grave of a smith.

The crossing of the barrier between life and death is associated with fear, hope, sadness, and belief - most of which generally defy reason. This is unfortunate in that 'reason' is all we can safely apply to the problem as to why someone is buried with one object in preference to another. The only starting point we have – our point of reference - is that the buried item must have held some meaning in life for the user and/or those who buried the deceased.

It is common to assume that grave goods must be for use in an afterlife. Another view is that perhaps some grave goods were deposited simply because they were closely associated with the deceased – part of who they were and how they were regarded in life by their family and the wider community. Something worn or used daily was perhaps seen as inseparable from that person, even in death. Such feelings can owe more to emotion and a sense of loss than belief in an afterlife.

The vast majority of Anglo-Saxon burials are those of 'workers' as any social structure can only maintain a comparatively small ruling elite. Consequently, most individuals would have used tools of some type and would have possessed multiple skills even if they had one main skilled occupation.

Metalworking – i.e. blacksmithing in all its manifestations - was a craft that was not open to the general population. Anecdotal evidence suggests that the smith may have been treated differently in death from other members of society and an aim here is to speculate as to why this may have been so.

Tools versus Dress Artefacts

In cataloguing finds; archaeologists must make decisions as to what does or does not constitute a tool. In most cases the decision is quite easy, while in a few instances the distinction is less clear. There is a tendency to classify a non-descript or unusual iron object as a 'tool' on the basis that it defies attempts at alternative classification. In collating the tool finds here, non-descript items have been discounted.

Preliminary analysis shows that female graves are more likely to contain one or more tool, usually spindle whorls or shears. The reasoning behind this is expanded upon later (p.21) but it can be posited here that the inclusion of those items in the burial acts as a "definer" for the individual concerned. Some of these objects are both dress items and tools, and may also indicate status or skill at the point of death. Some graves contain items identified as nails without any real context: these may in reality be tools, but have been discounted here as they may have served as charms,

---

[14] Hinton, 2000

protectors, scribes or fingernail scrapers. Many are damaged or worn, and generally too small to be used as awls or punches.

The finds are classified by find-spot (cemetery) with a breakdown and analysis - this is not often easy as the tool-related finds within cemeteries only account for a small percentage of the accompanied inhumations. However, in those few cemeteries- notably Blacknall Field Pewsey (Wiltshire),[15] Alton (Hampshire)[16] and Finglesham (Kent)[17] with a higher than average number of tool-related grave goods, it is possible to undertake some minimal statistical analysis. Some evidence is the "lack of evidence" and here it contributes to the overall picture.

As a general preliminary observation, in the main the tool finds from female graves are textile related.

---

[15] Annable & Eagles, 2010
[16] Evison, 1988
[17] Hawkes & Grainger, 2006

2 The Anglo-Saxon Smith

Status

Before we start to examine the role of the smith in Anglo-Saxon society, I can do no better than quote Motz: [18]

> *The craftsman who works in metal holds in certain cultures a very special position. The act of forging tools and weapons which help men in their survival is viewed in certain stages of social development in awe and fear and mystery, and the artisan in metal appears to be able, in surpassing human powers, to release the secret springs of creativity. It is therefore not surprising that the figure of the blacksmith found entrance into the fairy tales, folktales and mythologies of many lands, and that he plays a role in the rites of folk tradition.*

From this first paragraph, Motz's prodigious work and a series of archaeological finds, we have information about how the world of the Anglo-Saxon smith may have looked.[19]

Many occupations were essential to the health and wealth of Anglo-Saxon society but the metalworkers craft was the most technologically advanced. Metalworkers could transform ore from the ground into sparkling steel. In a world of simple energies, the power of spark and starlight rested in his hands. To some the process seemed a magical one – a power bequeathed by the gods.

From what can be gathered of the early Anglo-Saxon period (5th-7th century AD) many smiths were, for at least some of the year, peripatetic figures - itinerants travelling from one village to the next, with many villages in their domain, each individually too small to keep them fully employed. It is probable that most of these smiths had a permanent family home and workshop from which they traded. Family members would have been able to sell items while the smith was away travelling around a circuit similar to the king's *iter* or predicted visiting pattern.

The very fact of being a 'traveller' set the smith apart from many of his customers, making him a bringer of news and gossip, and no doubt stories of the road. He was a craftsman with a rare skill required by the village but separate from it: an outsider, a half-trusted wayfarer and one with an enviable power over iron and spark. Each settlement was dependent upon the smith to a greater extent than he was dependent upon a single village – and this asymmetry of need could, for some, add to the suspicion and 'darkness' surrounding his craft.

---

[18] Motz, 1983
[19] Hinton, 2000

2 The Anglo-Saxon Smith

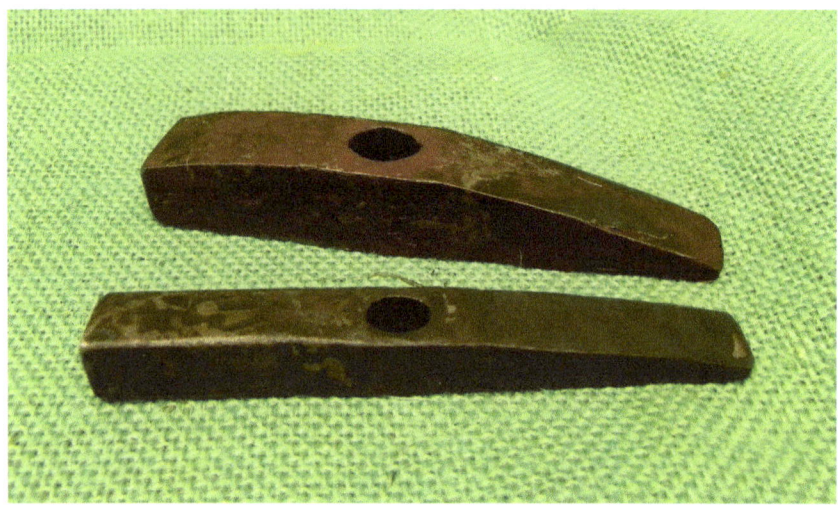

Figure 3 Reproduction hammer heads - the iron fists of the smith.

Smiths probably had one or more apprentices, for the smith's work was hard and a long road was best travelled in company. There were also times when an injured man required a helper. The find from Tattershall Thorpe[20] suggests the presence of an apprentice.

As knowledge is power, and it often provides a means for earning a living, it is probable that most craft skills were passed down through families. So a smith's apprentice would likely be a son or other relation.

The exact status of the smith is more difficult to ascertain. The itinerant smith was likely a freeman, entitled to go where he chose. Every village without a resident smith probably had a site for a smith to shelter, work and store his fuel.

There is evidence that the movement of a smith could be restricted, as his ability to forge weapons would make him a valuable military asset. Some may have been restricted to their own tribal or familial areas as a necessity, at least during the early Anglo-Saxon period. So, despite the powers and mystery sometimes attributed to the smith, he was, like other craftsmen, subject to the will and interests of those who ruled.

It is reasonable to suppose that most smiths were skilled in making and repairing household and farm related implements. As with all crafts there were a few with exceptional skills who were able to make fine work that was beyond the ability of village and town smiths. Many of these specialists were retained full-time by a lord or king (secular leaders and military organisers) who needed their skills to provide top quality and beautifully decorated war gear, which included arms, armour, buckles and horse gear. Such smiths, and their skills, were widely respected and the items they produced regarded as awesome. A smith of this calibre was truly a cunning man (*searuman* in Old English).

---

[20] Hinton, 2000

Left-Handed Craftsmen

There is evidence to suggest that smiths were often or generally left-handed, which is to say that they struck with the hammer held in the left hand. Various finds allude to this possibility, including some from Tattershall Thorpe where some of the tools have either been designed for left-handed use or simply used left-handed (as the wear burrs indicate).[21] We have no way of telling if the Anglo-Saxons had any preference or applied any social significance in left- or right-handedness. It is quite feasible that a man's handedness was looked upon as a random factor, since the right hand was called *seo swiðre hand* 'the stronger hand' and the left *seo wynstre hand* 'the weaker hand' – which is generally true of most human beings. We do not know of any "sinister" connotations with being left-handed at this time, but the remarkable number of left-handed tool finds could suggest that left-handedness was a requirement for the job of metalworker. Perhaps it was a sacred indicator of the smith's divine power? This is speculation but the subject would repay a detailed investigation..

The lack of tool finds from cemetery sites suggests that no smiths were buried with their tools within cemetery confines. This, combined with the fact that the Tattershall Thorpe smith and his tools were buried outside the cemetery confines,[22] has led some to suggest that in death the smith may have been treated differently from 'normal' men. Of course, one find does not provide evidence for an entire belief system. If further research and future finds indicate that smiths were routinely buried outside the confines of the public cemetery, then perhaps most cemetery sites may have a smith buried outside the perimeter – and for superstitious people, the further away the better!

In summary, we can follow Motz and suggest that some Germanic smiths were seen as outsiders; powerful and dark figures possessed of arcane knowledge; part man, part magician and feared for their unworldly skills. For these reasons, all or some of them may have been denied burial alongside the general population.

Evidence for Left- and Right-Handedness

An interesting aspect of tooling, often overlooked, is that of 'handedness', which is to say the hand in which the tools are designed to be used. Many tools can be used in either hand - hammers, chisels, saws and the like - while other tools cannot, such as scissors and tinsnips. An exception to this rule is shears, which can be used in either hand independent of their construction - a left-handed pair of shears works just as well used in the right hand. In that respect shears are anomalous and require further investigation.

Handedness in the modern general population of Western Europe (including the United Kingdom) is assessed as:[23]

    Left Hand Dominant: 10%   Right Hand Dominant: 90%

---

[21] Hinton, 2000
[22] Hinton, 2000
[23] Franks, 2007

Research into handedness is inconclusive as to why a person should favour using one hand over the other. There may be a genetic component in that the LRRTM1 gene determines handedness, but environmental factors also influence the preference of the individual. To illustrate this, I write and forge iron left-handed but I am a natural right-hand user; a short-term injury to a finger of the right hand during childhood forced an adaptation to work left handed even after the injury healed, a case of nurture taking precedence over nature.

We shall return to the matter of left- and right-handed tools below (p.29) when we consider the evidence for shears.

Dead Man's Tools

An artisan has a relationship with his tools that transcends death (in a loose sense) and this may help explain the lack of tool finds within burials of the general Anglo-Saxon population. There has been a long, if somewhat informal, tradition among tool-users to pass on their tools to those who may make good use of them. I hail from Sheffield, a place very familiar with the custom of "dead man's tools" used in the steel works and engineering workshops of the Don Valley. I have a fine collection of dead man's files of supernatural strength! These tools are much prized for two main reasons – firstly, they are a gift and, secondly, they are usually of the finest quality. As an old engineer has honed his skills and collected the best tools available to him over his life, so the tools are treated with reverence. However, with the recent demise of heavy traditional industries, this practice is no longer widespread but it does show a tradition of passing on tools from one generation to the next. In Anglo-Saxon times, tools may have had a strong 'heirloom' association above ground - as opposed to the heirloom tradition below ground with graves containing trinkets and keepsakes of various periods which make dating such a problem.

The passing of tools and knowledge from father to sons – from master to apprentice – may have been part of smithy ritual. An elderly or crippled smithy who was unable to work at his craft would have no use for the tools of his trade and would probably gain much psychological comfort from knowing they would be used by his successors. In a similar fashion his successors would perhaps 'feel' the power of ancient tools. Better surely to keep the tools alive than to bury them, except of course when there is no successor.

Anglo-Saxon Burial practice

It is not intended here to delve into the complex world of burial practice at any great length, for we need cover only the essentials of what we know. The Anglo-Saxons mourned their dead, as is shown in the care taken in the burials. Sometimes false beds were made for the dead,[24] and sometimes the graves lined with reeds and grasses. And of course in the pagan period the dead were buried with artefacts (grave goods). We do not know why objects, including weapons and tools, were placed in graves but it

---

[24] Speake, 1989; Penn, 2011

may suggest belief in an afterlife and the need to provide the deceased with things they had owned in life. The items buried with them seem to have reflected their place in society during their earthly life and possibly after it.

The artefacts in the grave were chosen by the living community that performed the burial. We can presume there were customs relating to both the burial of artefacts with the dead, and the distribution of property and personal items to the living. There was probably also some freedom for the deceased to determine which items of property went to the grave and how other items were distributed. In the early period these wishes would have been expressed in a verbal will – a spoken declaration of some kind.

The age of the deceased at death seem to play a part in the funerary rite, with status within the family and wider community reflected in the grave goods.

Interpretation of Cemetery Finds: The Acquisition and Use of Artefacts

The artefacts contained in a burial were of importance to someone, otherwise they would not have been included. They were of importance to the family organising the burial and in varying degrees to the deceased and their community. Likewise, items not included could be important for a number of other reasons – though this is more speculative and more difficult to ascertain. Halsall, in his research into the cemeteries of Merovingian Gaul, noted that specific female grave goods are more visible in burials of females aged from puberty to the early forties, in the context of dress items.[25] Härke's work also shows, in his study of Anglo-Saxon burials, that similar trends exist for male graves, although the relationship is more complex.[26]

My own research on tool burials show that a marked 'cut off' seems to present itself around the thirty-five years age group in female tool depositions - specifically in spindle whorls and shears. Although they have not been – but perhaps should be – regarded as dress items in the normal sense, this research indicates that they are, at the very least, female status markers indicating that the female to which they belong is in her peak productive years as a worker. This may correlate with her higher status within the family and community as a provider of cloth. As with other markers, after this age the tools begin to be omitted from burials, with the possible implication of her loss of status within the community due to a deterioration in her ability to manufacture cloth, making her more dependent upon those who continued to be productive; in this respect, the tool is an "ability to work" marker.

Not all female graves in the under thirty-five age group contain spindle whorls and shears. Speculation about the reason for this has included the suggestion that such items were passed on as heirlooms. Yet results from comparisons of cemetery sites hint at regional variations, as some are tool-rich and some devoid of any tool artefacts. Not every inhumation contains a spindle whorl or shears; this does not

---

[25] Halsall, 1996, 17-20
[26] Härke, 1992,a 158

preclude these being a status marker, as with every type of artefact there is never a "set" pattern of items buried, but rather always variations upon a theme. The family of the deceased had to make a decision about what should be included in the grave furniture based on tradition, the expectations of contemporary society and the need of the living to preserve as much as would be socially acceptable of the belongings of the deceased to be retained for use by the living.

Tool deposition in male graves is almost non-existent with the exception of awls, whose distribution is not widespread. In all probability the awl was looked upon as a personal item with its inclusion in the grave inventory an insignificant and random event. From the evidence presented here, it is clear that tool finds proper (timber axes, hammers, chisels and the like) are not included in the male grave inventory. Why is this so? Here I quote directly from Hirst and Clarke:[27]

> *Tools are vanishingly rare in migration period Anglo-Saxon graves, though present in migration period settlements and Geake has suggested that the increased frequency of tools in conversion period graves may indicate a change in the social importance of the skills of certain craftsmen, leading to their tools being seen as useful funerary signalling devices.*[28]

This suggestion cannot be ruled out because the evidence shows no tool deposits in early period cemeteries. However, I put forward for consideration an alternative reason for the paucity of tool deposits: Tools were not seen as personal or status markers because they were not classed in the early Anglo-Saxon period as 'personal effects' but were rather the property of the family who used them. In this context, they are used much as "dead man's tools" discussed above and passed on from parent to child, from one generation to the next. The principle reason may be due to the intrinsically high value of tools during this period. In a burial context (as in life) a man requires only one knife and one spear, but his requirement for tools runs into many, perhaps dozens of separate items for even the simplest craft. Many such tools were hand-made to the user's requirements and possibly also to the user's design. Iron and steel tools were an expensive investment which enabled craft skills to be passed on within families. Craft skills and tools-of-the-trade enabled families to earn a living, thus the tools, and information about their use, would have been guarded and preserved by the family to whom they collectively belonged.

Placing a spear or knife in a grave was a loss but generally not as great as the burial of tools that a family used on a daily basis, which could render them impoverished overnight. This idea is of course speculative but there is support (albeit of a later period) for this theory in the tool hoard from Nazeing (Essex).[29] The Nazeing hoard (see p.13) consists of some fifteen iron and two copper alloy artefacts, all presumed to be the scrap collection of a metalworker with a deposition date somewhere in the 11th century. The oldest item in the hoard was an axe-head of Roman date, which

---

[27] Hirst & Clarke, 2009
[28] Geake, 1997, 9
[29] Morris, 1981

suggests that it had seen service for nearly half a millennium before being retired. This in turn suggests that tools were well looked after, used and repaired for literally centuries - which supports the hypothesis that generally tools were too expensive or valuable to bury.

The increase in tool burials in the conversion period may reflect the status of the user as Geake has suggested. Equally, this effect may be a product of the increased availability of iron and its products, which would facilitate the availability of "spare tools" for burial. Lastly, as Geake noted, early Anglo-Saxon cemeteries are sometimes poor in finds but their attendant settlements are not; the addition of data from Bloodmoor Hill, Carlton Coleville (Suffolk) in this paper attests to this statement.[30] The reason for the difference in tool deposition is due to popular avoidance of the cemeteries versus accidental loss in the settlement - with the settlement finds representing decades of lost tools.

If grave goods were meant to be used in an afterlife, the grave good evidence suggests that women were expected to spin and men were expected to do as little work as possible, hardly a fair division of labour!

The Smith's Grave at Tattershall Thorpe

This is a rare and interesting find[31] outlined below in the discussion and table. The Tattershall inhumation contains a broad, if incomplete, range of tools.

Figure 4 A selection of the tool reproductions based on finds at Tattershall Thorpe

---

[30] Tipper & Dickens, 2009
[31] Hinton, 2000

Tool finds from the Tattershall inhumation

#	Tool	Description
1	hammer head	Rectangular construction 450g, heavily burred
2	hammer head	Square section, slightly burred 150g
3	hammer head	Rectangular section slightly burred 33g
4	anvil	Rectangular top with perforation in one corner
5	tongs	Snub nosed jaws with wooden covered handles 220mm long (iron work)
6	metalworkers clips	300mm long, riveted construction with tapering arms
7	snips	Asymmetrical Scandinavian pattern
8	draw plate	Containing 5 holes of varying diameter with slotted back
9	punch	180mm long, 25mm diameter at the top tapering to a point
10	punch	Tapering rectangular bar 91mm long x (12x4mm section)
11	punch	Tapering rectangular section, 53mm long x (9x3mm top)
12	punch?	Tapering bar, rectangular at top, 46mm long x (9x4mm top)
13	punch	50mm long, max width 7mm, possibly socketed
14	file	Rectangular section, transverse teeth on all 4 sides 164mm long including tang (46mm) 14mm wide x8mm thick, attributed to a metalworker due to its size
15	file	Transverse teeth on all 4 sides, file length 26mm x 8mm wide x 4mm thick
16	file	Rectangular section, tang encased in wood with a slight bolster between tang & file, extant length 37mm x5mm wide x 1mm thick
17	burin	Length 32mm projecting from bulbous wooden handle
18	graver	Flat faced with projecting spike
19-21	knife blades	In various states
24	soldering lamp	Surviving section is boat like with 2 projecting feet
25-26	cones	Made of iron and possibly small cupolas for the melting of precious metal (unproved)

2 The Anglo-Saxon Smith

The Tattershall Thorpe grave contained the remains of a skeleton, bone, iron, glass and Romano-British coins.[32] Some tools appear to have been in boxes whilst others were probably wrapped in textiles or leather. Dating of the grave by Hinton puts it in the region of 660-670 AD on the basis of datable finds and at first glance it seems to be a burial of a metalworker and his tools. As Hinton states:

Although some of the tools in the Tattershall Thorpe assemblage could have been used in more than one craft, the anvil, tongs and snips are things that only a metalworker would have needed…… The Tattershall Thorpe assemblage is ambivalent: on the one hand the absence of some equipment that might be expected may be because the assemblage comprises items gathered from a work bench to represent their owner's craft, not because they were all he owned. On the other hand it may be all that an itinerant smith happened to have with him when he met his death.

Hinton further states that there would have been a limit to what the smith could have carried if he did not have a cart, and a traveller may well have been prepared to keep his kit to a bare minimum. If the smith were a bondsman, the presumption is that he was removed from his settlement for burial outside the confines of the graveyard used by all the other villagers, and inhumed in a remote spot. (If he were just an itinerant; the same logic applies). The burial appears to have been conducted with some reverence given the structure of the grave; the rites were probably not the actions of uninterested individuals. Hinton goes on to suggest that a smith was an outsider - in the sense of a wanderer (if itinerant) and also in the spiritual sense; the burial may therefore represent a sentiment that the smith should be isolated in death and most of his equipment not used by others. But it is difficult to draw firm conclusions from the evidence of one burial.

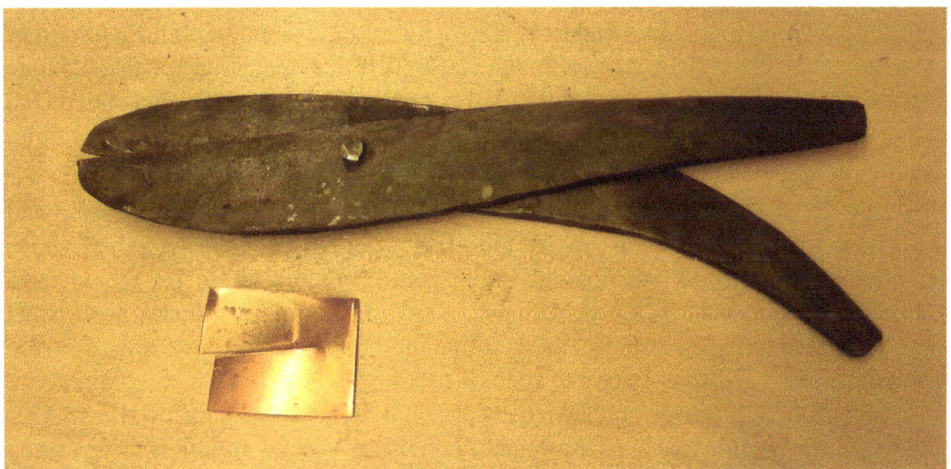

Figure 5 Reproduction of the right-handed shears from Tattershall Thorpe

---

[32] Hinton, 2000

Given Hinton's analysis of the grave one can put forward a number of ideas based on general smithing knowledge which, in some part, adds to the debate on this extraordinary find.

Finds 1 and 7 (the 450g hammer (1) and snips (7)) indicate that the deceased was left-handed; the deformation in the hammer face in the top right corner and the overall deformation of the face both attest to this, while the snips are of left-handed construction and would be very difficult to use right handed.

The weight of hammer 1 is sufficient for the manufacture of forged items commonly found in Anglo-Saxon graves, so it is entirely feasible that it is a smithing hammer. Hammers 2 and 3 are much lighter and show no left-handed use - which they should not as they are designed for light striking and struck with more precision so they would be generally used "flatter" on the work piece. Hammer 3, at 33 grams, is too light for any forging application while hammer 2, at 150 grams is suitable for hot forging work. I use a 200g hammer of similar construction for small finishing applications. Hammer 3 is likely to have been used for stamping and peening work on non-ferrous alloys, and I use a similar design and weight for this application.

The tongs (5) are on the small side for use with hot-worked material due to the danger of burning the hand, but they appear to have had wooden handle-covers which could extend their length. Even so they would be unwieldy for hot-working and it is more likely that the wood was for a soft-feel hard grip on cold materials - either ferrous or non-ferrous.

Hinton states that the punches numbered 10, 11, 12 and 13 may have been for metal stamping. In the light of the my own research, this is not only feasible but probable. Unfortunately no stamp impression now exists.

Find number 18, the graver, is a contentious piece. If we take the projecting spike as being original and not the product of corrosion, it is possible that it is a cold drill used for punching a hole in metal. It is a difficult tool to use but with the addition of the spike it could act as a locator in a centre-punch mark, making for the accurate positioning of a hole. Holes punched by this method give a very clean, round, flat finish but are limited in the depth of metal that can be punched, usually 1.5mm maximum.

Now turning our attention to the grave itself, we note that it is well constructed and the smith was interred with up to four boxes and additional wraps of tools, considerably more than one itinerant smith could possibly carry. He would have required a horse at least, or a cart. An interesting thing about the burial is not what is in it, but what is missing from it. I suggest that the smith may have had an apprentice (probably a son) and that given the state of tooling (not in the best condition at the time of burial) the burial contains the apprentice's tools or perhaps the smith's second set. Perhaps it was customary that upon the death of a smith his tools passed to his apprentice. It may also have been traditional to bury the smith with some of his tools so that he could continue his work in the realm of the dead.

Another explanation is that the smith died without heirs or an apprentice and all his equipment was buried with him.

The evidence from the cemetery sites listed in this report shows a lack of tool burials in male graves as either a matter of policy or of tradition, so it is not possible from this to know whether smiths were buried there or not.

There are other sites with tool hoards - notably Flixborough (Lincolnshire),[33] the Westley Waterless (Cambridgeshire) hoard[34] and the small hoard from Santon Downham (Suffolk), all of which were buried in cauldrons or vessels of metal and without any attendant inhumation. This would suggest that the burial of tools was made in containers for some specific reason which may have been the same as for the Tattershall Thorpe inhumation.

In summary it may therefore be concluded that:

1. In some cemeteries spindle whorls and shears are likely to have been included in the burial as female status markers. Those cemeteries that show such markers are not geographically distinct from those that have no markers.

2. Male graves of the 5th to 7th centuries contain no tools, for which three explanations suggest themselves:
   (a) that tools were not looked upon as personal effects and therefore not considered for burial;
   (b) that tools were the property of the family due to their intrinsic high value and therefore for use by the living and passed on from one generation to the next - in this context true "dead man's tools";
   (c) for reason of custom and/or superstition tools were not used as grave goods.

3. The change to an increase in male burials containing tools in the later conversion period may be due to a reduction in the cost of tools, therefore allowing the burial of such equipment without damaging the prosperity of the living. If there were social restrictions on burying tools (whether due to supernatural or other factors) it would imply that such restrictions diminished as the Anglo-Saxon period progressed.

---

[33] Evans, D.H. & Loveluck, C. 2009
[34] Fox, 1923

3 Tool Types in Anglo-Saxon Contexts

In the following, I have used evidence drawn from published archaeological reports relating to the Anglo-Saxon period. There are of course limitations in these data because (i) not everything that was buried survives to be excavated, (ii) not everything that is excavated can be identified accurately, and (iii) most of the evidence is taken from burials where the objects had been selected for inclusion in the grave, so they do not form a random sample. Therefore all the conclusions have to be treated with caution.

Shears

The manufacture of shears requires skill. They are difficult items to make, each blade requiring a slight inwards bend or "set" to allow the blades' edges to mesh together giving a single continuous cut line when in use. On a poorly manufactured set of shears – those with a weak spring action or badly meshing blades - the set is more pronounced, which causes the point where the blades touch to chip thereby disrupting the cutting motion. To alleviate this problem the shears can be opened up when not in use so the blades do not touch. This makes a determination of handedness difficult. The blades can also be unsprung and switched over, giving the impression that the blades are of opposite handedness (but only the set of the blades can help in indicating handedness). Alternatively, the blades can be forced fully closed by fitting a leather or fabric blade guard. In inhumation finds, this leaves us with a problem of determining the true handedness.

In calculating the statistics outlined here, indeterminate shears have been removed from the equation (i.e. shears that have been forced open or are too badly corroded to permit inspection) and all other results are based on the set and form of the blades at the time of excavation. The results show a startling revelation as to handedness.

From the excavation of the mainly 6th century cremation burials at Spong Hill (Norfolk) of the 22 shears displaying handedness, around 70% were left handed.[35] From the mid-5th to late 7th century Anglo-Saxon cemetery at Cleatham (Lincolnshire) of the 5 shears recovered 3 (60%) were left handed and 2 were right handed.[36] From the excavations of 5th-6th century material at Norwich Southern Bypass (Harford Farm, Norfolk) the figure was 50% for both right- and left-handed shears.[37] From the 5th-6th century Anglo-Saxon cemetery at Finglesham (Kent) the three shears recovered were all left handed.[38] From the 9th century finds at Coppergate, York only one pair of shears was recovered on which the preference could be determined, and that was left handed.[39]

---

[35] Hills, 1997
[36] Leahy, 2007
[37] Penn, 2000
[38] Chadwick Hawkes & Grainger, 2006
[39] Ottaway, 1992

3 Tool Types in Anglo-Saxon Contexts

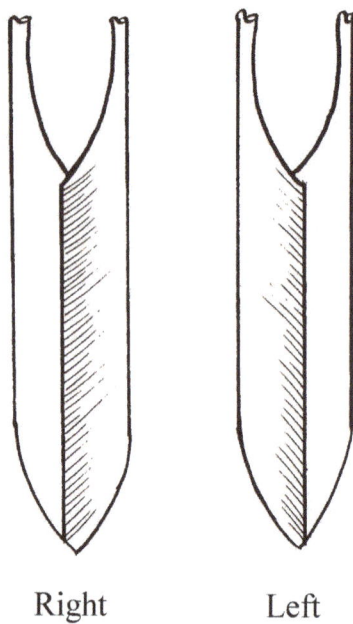

Right　　　　　Left

Figure 6 Ascription of handedness to shears.

If we cast our net further afield and inspect a site of the near Continent a similar picture emerges: in the Merovingian period (5th-6th century) cemetery at Goudelancourt-lès-Pierrepont (Aisne, France) the three shears recovered are all left handed.[40]

And finally, from the 14 Vendel graves in Sweden (550-790AD) of the four shears recovered all were left handed.[41]

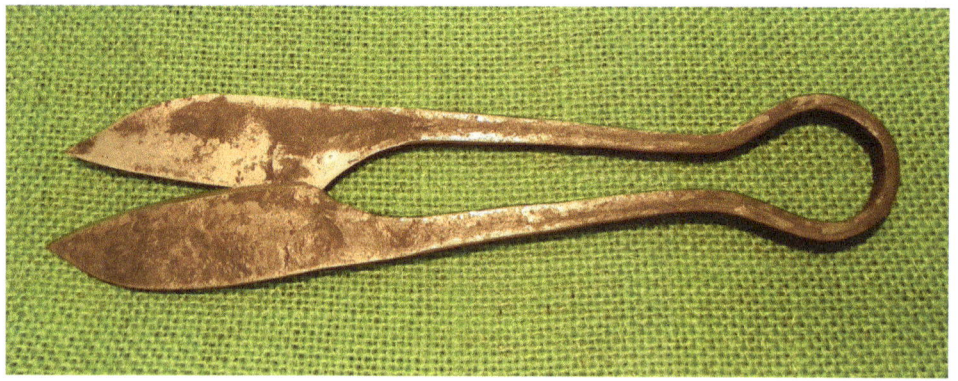

Figure 7 Reproduction right-handed shears.

---

[40] Nice,2008
[41] Ardwissen,1942

The results are startling in that for the majority of finds of shears (where handedness is observable) most are designed for left-handed use. A number of possible reasons may be advanced to explain this:

Tradition

A manufacturing tradition may exist whereby shears were generally made left-handed. This may have its roots in some aspect of pagan custom or belief. Equally the smithing of iron may have been a trade carried on by predominantly left-handed men; consequently most of the products they made were for left-handed use by habit. Given the nature of smithing and the position of smiths in society as somewhat strange and empowered with arcane knowledge, they may have specifically recruited left-handed apprentices to maintain a tradition. This is however purely speculative.

General Utility

Experiments have shown that shears can be used in either hand (unlike scissors and tinsnips) in which case making shears for either hand represents no technical problem. The primary use of shears was in the preparation of clothing and it may be that shears were designed predominantly for use in the left hand while the right hand was utilised for some other task. It has also been noted from practical experiments that if cloth is cut from right to left (as a right-handed user would naturally approach the task) using a left-handed pair of shears allows the user a clear view of the cutting line whereas using right handed shears masks it.

Ambidexterity

The early Anglo-Saxons were perhaps more often ambidextrous than the modern population. They may have been just as genetically predisposed to left- and right-handed behaviour as is the modern population. But the use of left-handed tools may have been encouraged as a matter of necessity. Any member of a society where a knowledge of medicine and of anatomy was limited could become a burden if the naturally favoured hand was disabled. Ambidexterity through nurture would enable a disabled individual to continue to contribute to society.

Accident of Manufacture

The chance manufacture of items left- and right-handed is possible. The human mind develops a set pattern and method of making things. Manufacturing important items such as tools with indeterminate or randomly-assigned handedness is highly unlikely.

Post Migration Cultural Change

It is also possible that the early Anglo-Saxon population demonstrated a higher degree of left-handedness than the modern population. There is some evidence that left-handed people are less averse to risk-taking than right-handed people, giving rise to a disproportionate number of Anglo-Saxon settlers with a left-handed preference. If this is so, the trend towards present levels of left-handedness could be attributed to the arrival of Christianity amongst the Anglo-Saxons during the 7th century. The church had strictures against left-handedness, it being considered sinister and corrupt, and attempted the eradication of this deviant behaviour through punishment.

Snips and Cutters

Anyone who has tried to use a pair of tinsnips in the wrong hand will quickly find that they will not work very well, even with modern high-tolerance tooling. Earlier snips perform even worse, so the handedness of their construction indicates the handedness of the user. Since the finds are rare the individual tools are discussed under metalworking tools (see below, p.48).

4 Tool Finds by Occupation

The tool finds are classified here by the occupation in which they are employed, rather than by findspot. This approach gives a more rounded picture of what has survived from each occupation or craft. Many tools can, of course, be used in more than one craft (the hammer, for instance) but a few are craft-specific in use.

The tools listed here are extant finds. Hones and knives are treated separately because these tools were used in every occupation. Knives are personal items, status-markers and general purpose tools; their analysis is restricted to the smaller knives of around 8" (200mm) overall length and shorter, and also included here are the more specialist craft knives rather than under their presumed occupational use. Hones as tools are often overlooked but are essential in maintaining a sharp edge on any cutting tool and are well represented, especially on occupation sites. They are however a rare find in inhumations and cremations where they are likely to represent a form of personal costume item.

The tool list is not exhaustive but contains examples of all the major tool finds and their variant forms. All the photographs show reproductions of the original item to display the tool in its pristine form rather than its usually corroded and nondescript excavated form.

Hones

For the purposes of this study both whetstones and hones are to be viewed as the same object class. A whetstone is used to create the edge of the blade, while a hone is used to add the final cutting face – to sharpen it when dull. The difference relates to function and to some extent to the fineness of the stone's grit, but they are both used for sharpening. We shall refer to both object types as hones in this study.

Excavated hones vary greatly in quantity from site to site, with many examples (mainly cemeteries) yielding few or no finds at all.

The size of hones does not vary greatly. In most cases they are designed to fit in the hand and to be easily transportable, usually as an item of personal kit. Larger examples are manufactured from larger pieces of stone and are likely to have a settlement context, i.e. a fixed location for their use and thus no need for portability. Since hones are recovered from many sites, only three are listed here. Each site yielded large quantities of hones (relatively speaking) so the size-spread within a grouping can be seen. As experiments have shown, a worn hone is much more useful than an unworn one since most hones would be used for a specific task such as the sharpening of knives or honing of needles. In the latter case, a groove is worn into the stone face; the groove makes the sharpening task easier and reduces the tendency of the work-piece to slip while in motion. This reduces the incidence of accidental injury.

4 Tool Finds by Occupation

Figure 8 Hones L to R, sandstone, slate and
the author's modern silicon carbide hone (heavily worn)

Hones can be broadly classified into two groups, primary and secondary. Primary hones are those mined and manufactured from virgin rock with the express intention of use as hones. Secondary hones are those made from processed stone, either re-used Roman stone, household stone or stone used for another purpose and converted to use as a hone, the classic example being reused quern stones.

In the Early Anglo-Saxon period it appears that the general practice was to use any suitable local stone to make hones.[42] At Sutton Hoo (Suffolk) an ornate stone bar was found, and an example from Hough on the Hill (Lincolnshire) with a carved human face tend to suggest that early period hones have an importance beyond that of mere utility.[43] This is supported by the discovery of a large hone (463mm long) found set upright near an early 7th century grave at Uncleby (Yorkshire).[44]

The smaller primary hones can be assumed to be personal items - though not necessarily in a funerary context. They are of uniform size, designed to fit snugly in the hand with no sharp edges. Hones are rare grave finds throughout the Anglo-Saxon period but increase in frequency somewhat towards the mid- to late-period. Since hone material is readily and freely available, one would feel that most burials would have them. Parallel to this is the lack of tool finds in early period burials -

---

[42] Leahy, 2007, 201
[43] See Mortimer & Pollington, 2013 for further discussion of this enigmatic object which may not have served as a hone.
[44] Smith, 1912

hones are a part of the toolkit and should be viewed in this context. The relative absence of hones and other tool types is presumably due to the preferences and customs of the burying communities.

The source of hones varies over time: in the early to mid-Anglo-Saxon period (up to the 10th century) hones are generally of local stones or derived from within Britain. Continental and Scandinavian hone finds in England are then quite rare and usually associated with Norse settlement or trade activities. However around the 10th century a sudden expansion in Scandinavian mining leads to an influx of foreign-sourced hones.

Finds from the London, Royal Opera House site, 600-900AD

Find No.	Period AD	Dimensions LxHxD mm	Remarks
S1	600-675	61x35x20	Fragment of sandy limestone possibly from Kent
S2	600-675	-------------	Fine grained quartz, stone reused for sharpening
S6	600-675	94x39x26	Sandy limestone
S17	675-730	164x71x37	Large hone made from greensand (surrey/Kent area), partially bored hole on the back side
S33	730-770	57x40x30	Extant size, made from micaceous sandstone
S41	730-770	190x?x116	Secondary hone, fine grained sandstone
S58	730-770	67x39x18	Possible hone, small fragment of sandy limestone
S85	730-770	120x111x41	Fine grained quartz sandstone
S89	730-770	-------------	Secondary hone, fine grained quartz sandstone
S156	770-850	133x59x36	Sandy limestone from the Kent/Surrey area, rectangular (nominally so)
S184	850-900	114x45x19	Complete quartzite sharpener, rectangular with rounded edges
S185	850-900	-------------	Pierced hone, the hole is a natural perforation, made from fine grained sandstone, wear patterns suggest made for a right handed user suspended from the left-hand side of belt

4 Tool Finds by Occupation

Finds from Carlton Coleville Anglo-Saxon Cemetery, 6th - 8th century AD

Find No.	Dimensions LxWxD mm	Remarks
295	32x43x20	Fine sandstone teardrop section rectangular bar, broken both ends
296	53x31x26	Micaceous sandstone, probably rectangular but only small fragments remain
297	70x50x34	Sandstone, triangular end fragment broken on both ends and face
298	53x51x40	Porous medium grained sandstone, irregular sub triangular in section, broken
299	126x58x46	Fine sandstone with a little mica, one side smooth, the others rough, large and tapering
300	119x64x15	Fine to medium sandstone crescent shaped and rounded
301	82x57x24	Sandstone with mica, tapering rectangular section, broken at one end and axially
302	42x35x4	Fine micaceous sandstone broken off fragment with rounded edges
303	45x58x24	Micaceous sandstone rectangular section, broken at both ends
304	138x87x25	Fine grained sandstone, large flattish sub rectangular piece
305	86x25x23	Metamorphic quartzite, rounded in section and at the ends
306	82x40x12	Metamorphic quartzite, rounded and worn
307	77x42x11	Metamorphic quartzite, rounded and worn
308	79x33x23	Metamorphic quartzite, oval sectioned and rounded
309	139x120x22	Sedimentary quartzite one flat and one rounded surface
310	93x39x17	Metamorphic quartzite, rounded rectangular bar, smooth and worn
311	107x53x25	Sedimentary quartzite rounded in section and at ends
312	126x67x23	Chalk, rounded, pitted and worn, possibly for polishing rather than sharpening
313	91x68x39	Fine grained limestone worked on one side only
314	85x35x18	Mudstone, possibly fine grained greywacke, rounded rectangular bar
315	57x39x30	Possible hone, fine grained mudstone, triangular with rounded edges
316	118x46x14	Dolerite, tapering and worn
317	91x78x16	Siltstone, irregular and rounded

4 Tool Finds by Occupation

The finds from Carlton Coleville contain both local and imported stone wares, the quartzite being relatively local and the others probably imported. The greywacke probably came from Wales, the Scottish uplands or Scandinavia. The limestones from the English Midlands and the dolerites from northern England, Scotland or Scandinavia. The sandstone, mudstone, limestone and siltstone examples are all 7th century in date with the quartzite and imported dolerite found in varying strata showing periods of trading between sites. There were no Scandinavian type schists or phyllites at the site, showing that there was no international trade in this region at this time (early Anglo-Saxon period) which agrees with finds from other sites.

Finds from Flixborough Anglo-Saxon Settlement 600-1000AD

Find No.	Date (century)	Dimensions LxWxD mm	Remarks
2333	8-9th	68x64x22	Coal measures sandstone, waxy deposit on surface, slab like, one face has more wear than the other, hone fragment
2334	8-9th	122x100x61	Limestone (Scunthorpe mudstones, basal part), sub rectangular block broken at both ends, sharpening stone.
2335	8-9th	27x24x8.5	Coal measures sandstone, bar shaped small personal hone, slightly tapered with both ends broken. Hone fragment
2336	Early 9th	40x27x20	Coal measures sandstone, bar shaped and tapered, broken at its narrower end. Hone fragment
2337	Mid 9th	100x83x33	Coal measures sandstone, covered on all faces with a waxy hard brownish deposit in places
2338	Mid 9th	101x46x14	Coal measures sandstone, bar shaped, used for point sharpening on one face, hone fragment
2339	Mid 9th	43x58x19	Hone fragment, coal measures sandstone, slab like and tapered at both ends, rectangular section
2340	9-10th	60x32x7	Hone fragment, sandstone likely from Southern Scotland or Cumbria
2341	9-10th	46x36x20	Hone fragment, coal measures sandstone, edges lightly rounded by wear
2342	Early 10th	27x42x32	Hone fragment with perforation (broken across perforation) sandstone, possibly millstone grit
2343	Early 10th	41x62x25	Hone fragment sandstone, possibly Wensleydale formation or coal measures
2344	10th	62x62x36	Hone fragment, sandstone upper carboniferous or middle Jurassic, possibly a tertiary used quern fragment, one edge of the hone has a dark brown-reddish deposit
2345	10th	55x45x12	Hone fragment, coal measures sandstone, contains small diagonal grooves
2346	10th	111x75x45	Hone fragment, coal measures sandstone, worked face exhibits a dark brown-reddish deposit
2347	10th	67x42x14	Hone fragment, coal measures sandstone, one face exhibits a dark brown-reddish deposit

The reddish-brown waxy deposits on the Flixborough hones are presumed to be caused by a fat used in the sharpening process. The colour is due to a suspension of iron particles in the fat.

The dating of the hones from Flixborough ranges from the 8th c. to a 12th -14th c. context. The majority are from the 9th-10th century, based on findspot and composition. No hones of Eidsburg schist were present indicating an Anglo-Saxon derived context (made from local stones). The Eidsburg schist is an import from the Telemark area of Norway and not generally seen before the 10th century when there was a marked increase in their export. Therefore the Flixborough sandstone hones are of an Anglian type.[45]

As a final word; the presumption is that the coarse hones (whetstones) are used for primary working and the finer-grained hones used for finishing and final sharpening.[46] This is evidenced in that most small personal hones are generally of a fine-grained type designed for maintaining the edge on tools.

Knives

Knives are multi-purpose tools with a wide variety of uses, so it is virtually impossible to determine any precise use for a specific knife. However, there are some specific Anglo-Saxon knife designs that imply a primary function. The three types are serrated, folding and pivoting.

Within the folding and pivoting knife groups ascribing a certain function is not easy. Findspot location and archaeological context can be helpful in this regard. Ottaway developed a typology based on five knife-blade types (A to E) with subsequent sub-categories.[47] Listed here are the three common knife types found from the Anglo-Saxon period, from both occupation sites and burials.

Figure 9   Principal AS.
blade profiles (after Ottaway)

Type A (top) Angled straight back blade (broken back type)

Type B (middle) Angled concave straight back blade, scooped forward edge

Type C (bottom) Convex back sloping towards the blade point

---

[45] Ellis, 1969
[46] MacGregor, 1982
[47] Ottaway, 1992.

4 Tool Finds by Occupation

Ottaway further suggests that the form of Type A knives – traditionally associated with the early to middle Anglo-Saxon periods - has its roots in Roman knife designs. By the Anglo-Norman period (late 11th – 12th c.) this knife style is superseded by other types (B, C).

Knife construction is often complex with quite a few manufacturing variations. The typology outlined by Tylecote based on construction details can also be applied to other edged tools.[48]

Class	Construction
0	all iron construction, no steel
1	steel core with an iron sheath
2	steel edge on an iron body
3	piled iron/steel construction (laminated)
4	steel sheath wrapped around an iron core
5	all steel blade

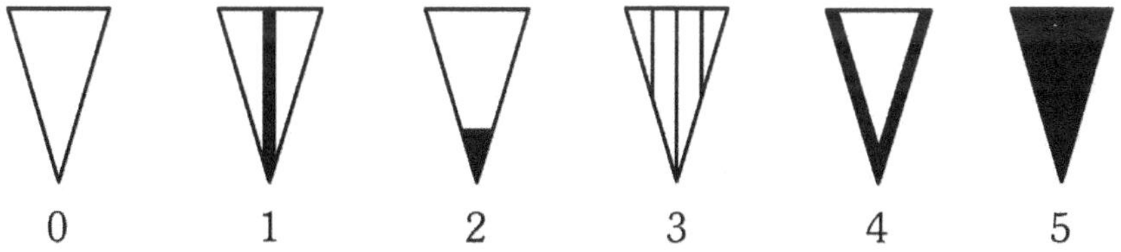

Figure 10 Iron/steel blade format (after Tylecote)

A good knife was valued by its user to the extent that after many years or even decades of use it became worn through re sharpening. A number of knife finds attest to this - for example, knife 6 from Anglo-Norman London, along with knives 16 and 17, all show extensive wear on the blade which is worn down past the tang.[49] From Coppergate, York,[50] comes a heavily worn knife (find 2279) dating from the mid-9th to the early 10th century, attesting to a long period of use and favoured retention by its owner. Some of the other Coppergate knives show varying degrees of wear, and indeed most occupation sites show knives having had extensive use over a period of time.

The size of knives varies due to function, with the smaller knife blades being more suited to intricate work, and personal hand knives being in the range of 10 to 15cm. Knife analysis from Fishergate, York, shows the smallest recovered knife to have a 40mm blade length (find 5004) presumed to be for use in bone and antler working, with 64% of the Fishergate knives in the size range 45-85mm and generally thought of as having craft applications.[51]

---

[48] Tylecote & Gilmour 1986
[49] Vince, 1991.
[50] Ottaway, 1992
[51] Rogers, 1993

Serrated Knives

A number of occupation sites contain knives with serrated blades, the presumed function being for sawing principally bone and antler. From Fishergate, York[52] comes knife 5014 with an extant blade of around 10 cm with fine serrations. Likewise a serrated knife from Coppergate, York[53] (find 2983), a knife of 13 cm length (including tang) which is of unusual construction in that the blade terminates in a flat end: this is deliberate and is a possible indicator that the blade was used two-handed with one hand holding the handle and the thumb and forefinger pinching the blade's end to steady it in use. The flat face removes the problem of the user stabbing his fingers when the blade slips (as I can attest from practice with the reproduction). Serrated-bladed knives are an intermediate step between knife and saw, but since they have no set to the teeth the depth of cut is limited because the knife body will bind in the cut. This may explain the number of antler tines recovered that have been scored around their perimeter and snapped off for further working. Serrated knives have multiple functions in a bone and antler working context, not only for sawing but for grooving and rasping the bone and antler.

Folding Knives

A further type is the folding single-bladed knife with examples from Coppergate (York), Thwing (North Yorkshire) and London. The examples from Coppergate are interesting. Find 2975 is not dissimilar to a modern penknife. The blade is small at around 5cm in length and may have been set in a wooden handle. Finds 2979 and 2981 are of a complex and unusual design in that they have scale plates of iron and a built-in awl protruding from the back of the handle with the folding blade at the front: a leatherworking function is likely for this class of knife. Akin to the Coppergate awl-knives is an example from Thwing (SF1983.46)[54] dated to the 8th or early 9th century, with the awl as an extension of the scale plates of approximately 17cm length: a leatherworking use for this knife is also likely although, for both the Coppergate and Thwing knives, bone and antler working purposes cannot be ruled out. A similar find was also excavated at Carlisle cathedral,[55] dated to the 9th or 10th centuries. Finally, an iron folding item (M249) was recovered from the Middle Saxon deposits at the Royal Opera House, London[56], which might be a knife or razor.

---

[52] Rogers, 1993
[53] Ottaway, 1992
[54] Ottaway, 1992
[55] Carlisle Archaeology Unit, Sf 218
[56] Malcolm, Bowsher & Cowie, 2003

4 Tool Finds by Occupation

Pivoting Knives

The final class of knives with a presumed specific craft application are the pivoting knives, of which a number of examples have been recovered from occupation sites. Pivoting knives are in the main a two-bladed knife, each blade of a different length and profile. The shorter is generally a type A blade with the longer usually a type C. The blade assembly pivots on a point with a recess either side of the pivot which locates onto a pin. The use of this type of knife is attributed to both ecclesiastical and leatherworking sites. From Coppergate, York[57] come three knives, numbered 2976-8 of 10 cm, 12 cm and 16 cm blade-lengths respectively.

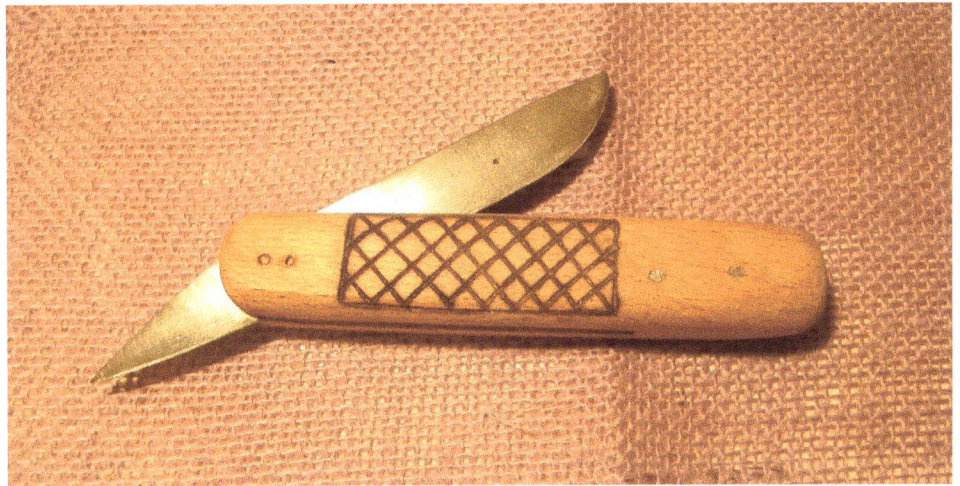

Figure 11 A reproduction folding knife of the Billingsgate, London, type.

From Billingsgate (London) come three knives (finds 18-20) dated to the 11th century; find 19 was complete and all three knives derive from a leatherworking context.[58] One pivoting knife was found in Canterbury (Kent)[59] with a presumed ecclesiastical context, and a similar knife was found at Little Paxton (Cambridgeshire).[60] Others have been discovered at Thetford (Norfolk),[61] Northampton[62] and Winchester (Wiltshire).[63] A fragmentary find from the settlement at Grove Farm, Market Lavington (Wiltshire)[64] (object number 5022, catalogue number 119), as reconstructed is in the region of 15cm long and 1.6cm wide, which is large for this type of knife. Finally, from the settlement deposits at Bishopstone

---

[57] Ottaway, 1992
[58] Vince, 1991
[59] Graham - Campbell, 1978
[60] Addyman, 1969
[61] Goodall, 1984
[62] Goodall, 1979
[63] Biddle, 1990
[64] Williams & Newman, 2006

(East Sussex) comes a pivoting knife (find number 43) from a 9th - 11th century context, of approximately 100mm in length (as reconstructed).[65]

Another type of pivoting knife comes from the Anglo-Saxon cemetery at Blacknall Field, Pewsey (Wiltshire) (grave 27, dated to 475-550 AD), a bone-handled knife (partially damaged) with a single blade with a central pivot and two holes, one at each end, that allow the knife edge to be swapped over by the removal of the locking rivet.[66] The construction of this knife suggests that it was originally designed to present a fresh, sharp blade for use rather than reversed when the original blade was worn out. Since the balance and design of the knife suggest it was made as one piece and shows no sign of wear, the pivot system was intentional and designed to be used.

The exact uses of these knives are open to debate but Biddle suggests that knives of the Canterbury design are manuscript scalpels. In the case of the Canterbury find this may be so because the bone scale plates are ornately carved, but other extant finds fit in well with a leatherworking context.[67]

Metalworking Tools

By far the greatest diversity in tooling occurs in metalworking, which would seem obvious given that many other tools are manufactured from iron and steel. As ever, the extant finds are a poor reflection of what must have originally been available to the Anglo-Saxons. Our sources of information are burials, casual losses and occupation sites, but nevertheless a good array of finds present themselves.

Hammers

Since all tools were handmade, they were manufactured to the requirements of the customer alongside the ability of the smith. Each one was effectively a one-off item. They were all made to the same basic patterns, but this does allow for variations in most every aspect of the actual design. Hammers are quite rare finds - listed below are the principal known hammer finds from Britain during the Anglo-Saxon period.

The larger hammers conform to a standard design of square or rectangular section with the punched hole at the highest (thickest) point tapering gently to the main face and steeply to the tail face. This seems to be the standard hammer shape for the early medieval period for all of Europe with even the Mästermyr hammers conforming to this basic design.[68]

The larger hammers of 600g plus are general forging hammers suitable for most manufacturing operations. The hammers in the 400g category are light ironworking or non-ferrous metalworking hammers. The smaller hammers are for general craft work or specialist metalworking. The lightest hammer recovered from an Anglo-Saxon context was the 33g hammer from the smith's grave at Tattershall Thorpe[69]

---

[65] Thomas, 2010
[66] Annable & Eagles, 2010
[67] Biddle, 1990
[68] Arwiddson & Berg 1983
[69] Hinton, 2000

4 Tool Finds by Occupation

and, given the context of the finds, was probably used in fine metalworking as was the hammer from the Nazeing hoard.

The hammer from Knoc-y-Doonee, Isle of Man[70] is from an early Viking boat burial of some status and was found along with a pair of tongs giving rise to the notion that the items were of some ritual significance. Most Anglo-Saxon hammers are of square or rectangular section but the hammer from Coppergate, York (find 2203) is oval in section. Round and oval sectioned hammers are quite rare but there are examples from the Byglands smith's grave (Telemark, Norway) and the riveting hammer from the Mästermyr hoard (Gotland, Sweden). Some Roman examples are round in section, especially the larger sledgehammers now in the collection in Lincoln museum.

No sledge hammers are known from an Anglo-Saxon context (generally over 2000g weight) but these would be confined to the primary forging of bloomery billets and are not likely to be found in occupation contexts.

The question of whether hammer faces were steeled or not is as yet unresolved. Deformation patterns on the large Coppergate hammer (2201) and the hammers from Tattershall Thorpe would suggest that it is unlikely – or, at least, if the faces were steeled they were unhardened. Steeling is not required for ironworking since iron at 1000°C is much softer than iron at 40°C and I have used mild steel forging blocks that show little wear after many thousands of hammer blows working hot steel.

Find No.	Weight grams	Length mm	Head mm	Tail mm	Site	Date
1	450	115	30x20	30x10	Tatershall Thorpe[71]	690AD
2	150	110	20x20	20x5	Tattershall Thorpe	690AD
3	33	70	10x10	10x2	Tattershall Thorpe	690AD
2201	658	110	40x40	40x16	Coppergate[72]	10/11thC
2202	---	---	---	---	Coppergate	10/11thC
2203	75g*	80	8x10 oval	14x2	Coppergate	10/11thC
---	650	120	30x20	15x20	Thetford[73]	9/11thC
---	100g*	95	15x15	15x5	Soham[74]	---
F	450g*	125	25x30	---	Isle of Man[75]	"Early Viking"
12	--	115	13x8	13x6	Nazeing Hoard[76]	10thC deposit

---

[70] Kermode 1930
[71] Hinton, 2000
[72] Ottaway, 1992
[73] Goodall, 1984
[74] Wilson, 1976
[75] Kermode, 1930
[76] Morris; 1983

4 Tool Finds by Occupation

Figure 12 A selection of reproduction hammers

Anvils

Anvil finds are unfortunately very rare, with only two currently known. One find is from the smith's grave at Tattershall Thorpe of rectangular construction, 100 mm high with a slightly domed top, larger than the body of the anvil and measuring around 76x60 mm with a slot in one corner as a punch-hole; it weighs 940g and is dated to around 690AD.[77] The second find is a smaller bick anvil from Coppergate, York (find 2200) dated to 930-975AD, 80mm high and 20x10mm rectangular in section with a flat bick head some 50mm long.[78] At the back of the head are three transverse grooves in the metal which possible indicates use as a needlemaker's anvil. Ottaway discusses the possibility that the grooves form part of a swaging block, but this seems unlikely given their small size.[79] Metallographic investigation shows that the anvil was made from a mixture of ferritic and phosphoric iron, the principle product of the bloomer furnace, and that the beak of the anvil showed evidence of cold working.

---

[77] Hinton, 2000
[78] Ottaway, 1992
[79] Ottaway, 1992

4 Tool Finds by Occupation

Anvil finds from Continental Europe at this time are much more numerous with four anvils recovered from the Mästermyr hoard (Gotland)[80] and one from the Bygland smith's grave (Telemark, Norway).[81]

The main requirement of an anvil is to be heavier than the hammer that strikes it. This does not preclude stone anvils from use at this time and large stones recovered from occupation sites may have been used in this way, but petrographic analysis might not discern any tool function or use. It is interesting to note that an Iron Age find from the River Lea at Waltham Abbey (Essex)[82] dating from 100BC -100AD contains an anvil not dissimilar to the Coppergate example but more closely resembling one of the finds from the Mästermyr hoard alongside a hammer more akin to a modern lump hammer than the stylised Anglo-Saxon hammer types.

Figure 13 Reproduction of the Tattersall Thorpe anvil

---

[80] Arwiddson & Berg, 1983
[81] Blindheim, 1963
[82] James & Rigby, 1977

4 Tool Finds by Occupation

Tongs

Quite a few metalworking tongs exist from the Anglo-Saxon period: ten in total from a number of diverse sites. Tongs are generally large hot-metalworking pliers associated with primary metalworking functions such as forging and casting. They generally conform to the same structured norm, the one known exception being the tongs from the River Thames at London Bridge (Figs. 14 & 15) which are of a most unusual, if not unique, design with the reconstruction showing limited use for heavy work but suitability for hot working thin sheet.

Some of the finds are fragmentary but more than half the known examples are complete.

The tongs of note are the pair recovered from the Thames (investigated by Wheeler) of an unusual design in that the bottom jaws fold round the upper jaw when closed, totally encapsulating the 'blade'.[83] It has been suggested that these 'tongs' are in fact shears designed to cut hot iron sheet, although the experimental reconstruction presented here proved that the blade was incapable of cutting 1mm thick steel plate at 900°C. Furthermore, the 'blades' are of insufficient mass to cut the metal without bending. The tool must therefore be classified as tongs, although the design only facilitates the holding of sheet metal. We do not know if the enclosed blade is "nicked" for holding wire but this should be investigated as this design of tong would be well suited to that operation.

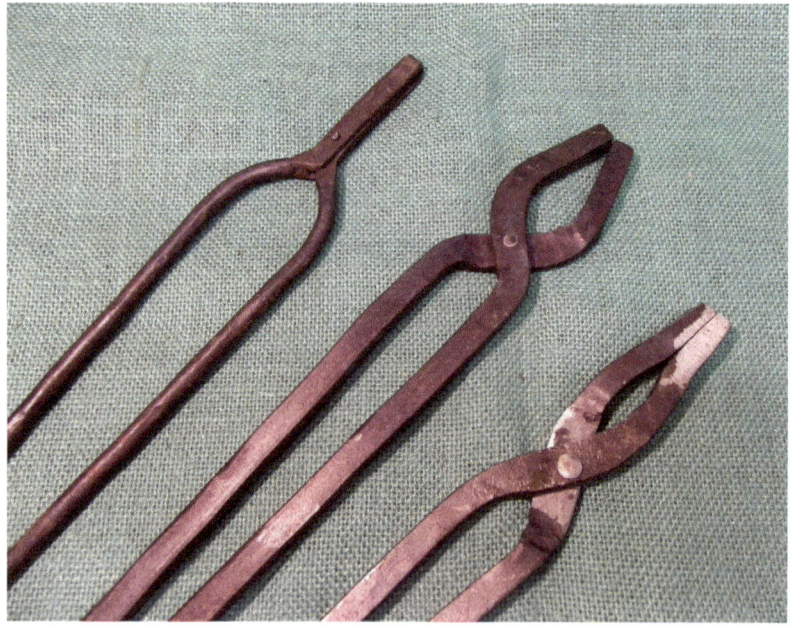

Figure 14 Reproduction tongs left to right:
London Bridge, Knoc-y-Doonee, Tattershall Thorpe

---

[83] Wheeler, 1927

4 Tool Finds by Occupation

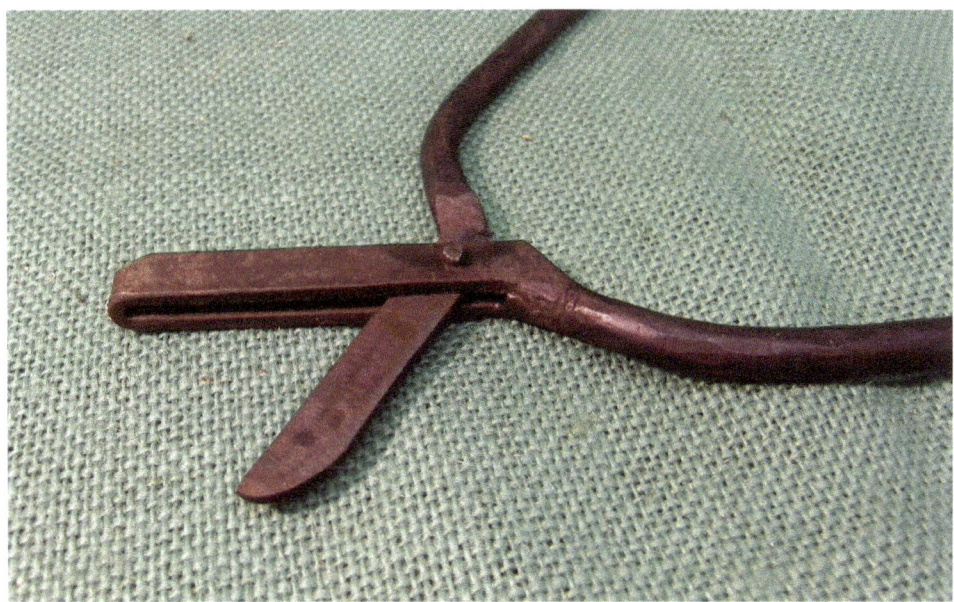

Figure 15 The London Bridge tongs

Date	Length	Site & remarks
11thC	28cm	Anglo-Norman London, find 21[84]
11thC	28cm	London, Enclosed blade design[85] (MoL,A23506)
690AD	22cm	Small Tongs from Tattershall Thorpe[86]
Mid 9thC	16cm	Flixborough[87] find 3063
Viking	38cm	Knoc-Y-Doonee[88] Isle of man Viking occupation
---	---	Sibertswold[89]
---	18cm	Shakenoak[90] Kent (AN1970.466)
8-9thC	---	Ramsbury[91] Wiltshire 2 pairs fragmentary
770-850AD	---	Middle Saxon London[92] find M277 fragment

---

[84] Vince, 1991
[85] Wheeler, 1927
[86] Hinton, 2000
[87] Evans & Loveluck, 2009
[88] Kermode,1930
[89] Faussett,1856
[90] Wilson, 1976
[91] Haslam, Biek & Tylecote, 1980
[92] Malcolm, Bowsher & Cowie, 2003

The size and shape of the tongs from Anglo-Norman London, although incomplete, would suggest that they are crucible tongs. The find from Flixborough (Lincolnshire) is unique from the Anglo-Saxon period in having an adjustable locking plate built into one arm, which allows for adjusting the tension on the material as it is worked. The tool could therefore be described as 'vice tongs' and is not likely to have been used on hot material. Many of the tongs are in the 18-28cm length which would, on the face of it, suggest a cold-working context, although experiments have shown that tongs of this length are usable in a hot-working context provided the smith wrapped his hand with a damp cloth.[93] The largest pair recovered was from the Viking boat burial on the Isle of Man at Knoc-Y-Doonee along with a hammer head. Given the context one would assume that this was a smith's set due to its heavy manufacture - in comparison the tongs from the Mästermyr hoard (circa 1000AD) are quite light in construction.[94]

Snips & Cutters

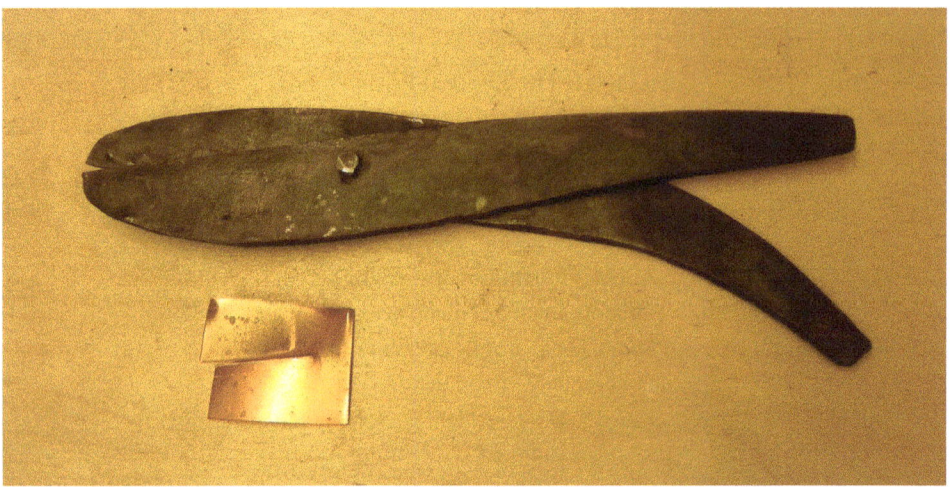

Figure 16 Tattershall Thorpe cutters reconstructed as a right handed pair and not left handed as the original

These two tools are effectively the same depending from an archaeological point of view. From the Anglo-Saxon period there are one possible and two definite finds. The first is a very fragmentary find from the settlement area at Bloodmoor Hill, Carlton Coleville (Norfolk) find 291, with only the rivet-hole and partial blade present.[95] The complete finds are (1) Tattershall Thorpe (690AD), find no 7, a pair of 183mm long asymmetrical left handed cutters of the same design as the pair from the Bygland smith's grave, with a similar find from the Mästermyr hoard and the grave at Herouvillette (France) (also left handed) indicating that asymmetrical pliers

---

[93] Authors own experiment at West Stow, Suffolk, 2011
[94] Arwiddson & Berg, 1983
[95] Lucy, Tipper & dickens, 2009

may represent the design norm for early mediaeval Europe.[96] The second pair are symmetrical, from Coppergate, York of 9th to 11th century date, nominally 200mm long with a curved handle to allow the blades to close when the handles are touching.[97] This pair of cutters is also left handed in design. As to why there seems to be an asymmetrical preference is unclear. Experiments have shown that constructing cutters asymmetrically is easier than making them symmetrical, as any slight deviation in the symmetrical design in either arm makes the cutters look odd, whereas with an asymmetrical design there is a degree of stylistic balance which may have been a desired feature. Reconstructions also show that the asymmetrical pliers fit easily into the hand which may add to the preference for such a design.

My reconstructions of the Tattershall Thorpe, Coppergate and Mästermyr cutters (also left handed) show that they are quite effective at cutting non-ferrous metals in the region of 1mm thickness (fully hardened) and 1.5mm thickness in the annealed condition. The only problem encountered in asymmetrical pliers is that they have no back-stop so the blades can cross over, and they also have a tendency to "nip" the hand when closing. Whichever design was employed, they were an effective cutting tool.

Files

Figure 17 Reproduction files.
Flixborough 3092 (top), Coppergate 2247 (middle), Coppergate 2248 (bottom)

---

[96] Decaens, 1971
[97] Ottaway, 1992

4 Tool Finds by Occupation

Files are an important tool of the fine metalworker. Workers in primary forging and manufacture have little need for these tools as their main function is the light removal of excess metal - usually a non-ferrous metal. The finishing of castings and intricate shaping are carried out with files. The examples listed here from a number of sites are presumed to be metalworking files due to the tooth frequency, where fine teeth indicate a metalworking use and coarse teeth indicate a bone, antler or woodworking context (these files or rasps are dealt with in the appropriate section).

Find Spot	Ref.	Date	Dimensions
Fishergate York[98]	4941	11th-12th c.	45 mm long including tang, rectangular construction 6-7 cm
Tattershall Thorpe[99]	14	690AD	161 mm long (46mm tang) fine-toothed rectangular construction
Tattershall Thorpe	15	690AD	102 mm long (including 26mm tang) rectangular 8x2 mm, teeth on all four sides
Tattershall Thorpe	16	690AD	Tang in wood, 5x1mm rectangular. 3 7mm extant blade length
Coppergate York[100]	2248	9th-11th c.	89mm long, no teeth to 1 5mm of each end, 1 side & 1 edge toothed, 6x2mm rectangular x 89 mm long
Coppergate York	2446	9th-11th c.	Four sides marked. 67 mm long 6x3 mm, rectangular section, fine-toothed
Coppergate York	2447	9th-11th c.	80 mm long, rectangular section, 10x2 mm
Flixborough[101]	3092	10th-11th c.	Fine toothed 16 teeth per cm. Length 64 mm, 6 mm wide
Flixborough	3093	unstratified	Remains of horn handle length, 62 mm 3x6 mm, rectangular section

Some of the files mentioned above contain small fragments of non-ferrous metal embedded in their teeth (principally Flixborough 3092 and Tattershall Thorpe 15) indicating their use as non-ferrous metalworking files. It should be remembered that any files containing an iron fragment will not show as any resultant oxidisation will match that of the file.

File construction on the whole seems to limit the file's cutting surface to one face, but sometimes one side is also cut and in rarer circumstances all four faces (e.g. Tattershall Thorpe 15 and Coppergate 2446). The lack of multiple-face cutting seems strange, since the file requires only one heat treatment or case hardening process with a four sided file lasting four times as long for the same amount of

---

[98] Rodgers, 1993
[99] Hinton, 2000
[100] Ottaway, 1992
[101] Evans & Loveluck, 2009

manufacturing effort. Set against this is the fact that most modern files have at least one edge that is smooth as a side protector to stop the file drifting sideways and damaging the work piece.

Experimental reproductions of period files have shown that they do not require great skill to manufacture, just a sharp small chisel and a steady hand.[102] The finer the file, the easier they are to make as each cut augments the profile of the preceding chisel cut to give an effective cutting edge.

Continental file finds are as rare as those from Britain. There are four files from the Mästermyr hoard (Gotland)[103] although two of these are more like rasps. One file was found in the Tjele (Denmark) hoard[104] and one file/rasp from the Birka (Sweden) graves.[105] One file was found in the 10th c. occupation site at Århus (Denmark)[106] and two files from the Bygland smith's grave (Telemark, Norway).[107] There is also another file from Britain discovered at Beverley (Yorkshire) on which I have no further information at the time of writing.[108] It is entirely possible that some of the extant rectangular section iron bars recovered from various sites may be very fine files and file cuts of 15 teeth per cm (tpcm) are achievable as experiments have shown.[109] It would require little rusting to remove all trace of such shallow chisel marks, making identification impossible. One possible example is that from the occupation deposits at Bloodmoor Hill, Carlton Coleville (Norfolk)[110] find 290, of file-like shape, 210mm long and 13mm x 7mm in section.

Chisels

Chisels can be broadly categorised as either hot- or cold-working tools. Hot chisels, being generally larger, are designed for the hot cutting of metal while cold chisels, as their name suggests, are for the cold cutting. Sizes can vary greatly with cold chisels as small as 25mm in length suitable (if not desirable) for the manufacture of files, whereas hot working equivalents are in the order of 150-200mm to protect the hand from the heat of the workpiece. Archaeologists generally clump together chisels and punches under the general heading of 'punches' so extant finds do require some "filtering" to provide a more specific label for individual tools. Cold chisels are quite an effective means of cutting sheet metal, especially for items too thick for cutters or snips. A good carbon steel chisel will quite easily indent a two to four mm cold iron plate to allow the plate to be bent and split, and will also allow for the cutting of quite complex shapes using the "crack and bend method" (i.e. partially cutting through the sheet and working it back and forth until it cracks). The chisel finds listed below are

---

[102] The smaller the chisel, the better - typically around 30 to 40 mm
[103] Arwiddson & Berg, 1983
[104] Munksgaard ,1984
[105] Arbman, 1940
[106] Anderson & Madsen, 1985
[107] Blindheim, 1963
[108] Goodall, in Armstrong, Tomlinson & Evans, 1992
[109] Author's own work, unpublished
[110] Lucy, Tipper & Dickens 2009

4 Tool Finds by Occupation

from a number of sites around Britain. The list is not exhaustive as it is not the intention to produce a gazetteer of finds; only those chisels in good condition have been included. Stray chisel finds do exist, but usually the main concentration is from occupation sites such as Coppergate York,[111] Carlton Coleville (the Bloodmoor Hill site)[112] and the Crayke hoard[113] in Yorkshire. The most unusual chisel context is grave 54 at Butlers Field, Lechlade (Wiltshire)[114] a female of 20-25 years of age buried with a large-bladed cold chisel, 110 mm long with a blade flaring out to 28 mm wide.

Area	Date	Find	Description
Crayke	950-1100	--	141 mm long x 14 mm wide rectangular
Crayke	950-1100	--	95 mm long x 14 mm wide rectangular
Crayke	950-1100	--	185 mm long 11 mm wide rectangular
Crayke	950-1100	--	154 mm long 16 mm wide rectangular
Fishergate	Early 8th c.	4939	100 mm long 20 mm x 10 mm section
London[115]	11/12th c.	22	89 mm long 12x12 mm rectangular; found at the waterfront bank
Coppergate	9th c.	2206	100 mm long 6x6 mm section
Coppergate	9th c.	2218	44mm long 8x6mm section, possible file makers chisel
Coppergate	9th c.	2208	140 mm long 10 mm diameter tapering to a flat chisel 10mm wide
Coppergate	975-11th c.	2245	80 mm long 10x5 mm section
London[116]	675-850	M89	110mm long x 10 mm wide at the point, rectangular section, Royal Opera House site
London	675-850	M140	60mm long x 10mm wide at the blade, rectangular section, Royal Opera House site
London	675-850	M121	90 mm long x 14 mm wide at blade, rectangular section, Royal Opera House site
Nazeing[117]	10th c, deposit	13	168 mm long, 20x19 mm head tapering to a flat blade, possible woodworking chisel
Carlton Coleville[118]	6-8th c.	283	50 mm long, 16x10 mm section at head
Carlton Colevile	6-8th c.	284	91 mm long, 16x14mm section at head
Carlton Coleville	6-8th c.	285	83 mm long, 13x10 mm section at head
Butlers Field Lechlade	5-7th c.	Grave 54	110 mm long tapering and flaring to 28 mm wide

---

[111] Ottaway, 1992
[112] Tipper & Dickens, 2009
[113] Crayke hoard discovered 1937 in Yorkshire. dated to 950-1100AD
[114] Boyle, Jennings, Miles & Palmer, 1998
[115] Vince, 1991
[116] Malcolm, Bowsher & Cowie, 2003
[117] Morris, 1983
[118] Lucy, Tipper & Dickens, 2009

4 Tool Finds by Occupation

Figure 18 Reproduction chisels, punches and the holes they make

Chisel construction is fairly simple, usually a square- or rectangular-section shaft tapering from the head to a flat blade. In some cases, such as Coppergate 2208, the shaft is round in section tapering to a flat blade. The blade is usually the same width as the diameter of the round body, as is also usually the case with the square or rectangular section chisels being no larger than the head and usually narrower. An exception here is the find from Butlers Field grave 54 which flares out from a tapered square section.[119] Given that it is from a female grave containing textile-related tooling, it is possible that it has a textile-related function, although this is speculative.

---

[119] Boyle, Jennings, Miles & Palmer, 1998

4 Tool Finds by Occupation

Punches

Punches, like chisels, can be used either hot or cold. Hot punches are generally larger than cold punches and are used for the punching of hot metal - typically eyes for hammers - and any other type of hole required in the metalworking process. Hot-working punches are either round, tapering to a point or square-section tapering to a round point. It is interesting to note here that the claw hammer recovered from Goltho (Lincolnshire) has a square hole for the hammer shaft indicating the use of square punches in its hot-working.[120] The smaller types of punch are used for a myriad of other functions such as the cold-piercing of thin sheet (both iron and non-ferrous) and the stamping of metals - again usually non-ferrous with repoussé dot work and more complex stamp work. Hines put forward the premise that:[121]

> "... the cutting of metal punches was a skilled, specialist occupation and therefore beyond the expertise of the average metalworker..."

This assertion is flawed as many cemeteries of the Anglo-Saxon period have punched metalwork finds, indicating that the distribution and use of punches was widespread. My own experimentation has shown that punches are easily manufactured by hand (in some cases, in just a few minutes) and that punched impressions, even using modern mild steel nails, can be used to yield a punch capable of producing stamp marks numbered in the hundreds. The skill needed to create the punch is minimal, to the extent that some of the less elaborate plate brooches could have been purchased blank and stamped by the user to their own design.

No decorative metalworking punches exist with their impression intact[122] but we are left with a large corpus of punched impressions in metalwork (of which a selection is listed in the appendix). Similar punch designs are repeated in many cemetery finds, but demonstrable use of the same punch on different items is very rare with only a few recorded instances. One example is an unusual double-spiral stamp used on a set of wrist clasps at Sleaford (Lincolnshire) which re-appears on work elsewhere in the cemetery.[123]

One of the punches used on the Mucking belt suite (Pl.9C, Fig.8.38) from grave 117 was also used on the quoit brooch found in grave 12 at Charlton Plantation and a stamp match was found on a pair of great square headed brooches from Little Wilbraham (Suffolk, grave 111).[124] On the basis of the lack of matching finds, Hines suggests that we have recovered only a tiny fragment of what was once in circulation. This is both plausible and probable, but equally it can be argued that punches were easily made and discarded, possibly used on just one or two items before being replaced.

---

[120] Beresford. 1987
[121] Hines, 1993, p85
[122] There is a stamp from the Mästermyr hoard (Gotland, Sweden) (number 84) now corroded but the accompanying lead pad(number 8)5 still retains the 'double triangle and three dots' impression
[123] Hines, 1993, p85
[124] Davies, Bojko, Crowfoot, Harding & Henderson, 1984; Inker, 2000, p.41

4 Tool Finds by Occupation

Area	Date	Find	Description
Crayke	950-1100	---	185 mm long x 20 mm wide, tapering to a point
Crayke	950-1100	---	152 mm long x 12 mm wide, tapering to a point
Fishergate[125]	Late 8th c.	4935	64 mm long 6x8 mm, rectangular, tapering to a point
Fishergate	Late 8thC	4936	64 mm long, 8x8 mm section tapering to a point
Tattershall Thorpe[126]	690AD	9	180 mm long, round section 2 5mm diameter, tapering to a point
Tattershall Thorpe	690AD	11	53 mm long 9x3 mm section, tapering to a point
Tattershall Thorpe	690AD	12	46 mm long 9x4 mm section, tapering to a half round
Tattershall Thorpe	690AD	13	50 mm long 7x7 mm section, tapering to a point
Coppergate[127]	9-11thC	2213	80 mm long 16x8 mm section, tapering to a point
Coppergate	9-11thC	2220	84 mm long, 10 mm diameter, tapering to a point
Coppergate	9-11thC	2210	44 mm long 8x4 mm section, offset point
Coppergate	9-11thC	2219	52 mm long 8x6 mm section, tapering to a point
Coppergate	9-11thC	2204	110 mm long, 14 mm square section at middle, tapering both ends
Carlton Coleville[128]	6-8thC	286	89 mm long 16x11 mm section, tapering to a point
Carlton Coleville	6-8thC	287	112 mm long 8x8 mm section, tapering to a point
Carlton Coleville	6-8thC	288	76 mm long 23x1 9mm section, tapering to a point
Mucking II cemetery[129]	5-7thC	Grave 923	a pair of nominally square sectioned punches around 80 mm long and 10 mm square

The punches listed above are for the non-stamping type, i.e. those in general use for making holes, repoussé dot work and light, simple decoration. The list is not exhaustive but shows the sizes of the punches recovered. There are notable punches that by their size and shape may well be for hot-metal working (for example, Coppergate 2204 and Tattershall Thorpe 9) but it is entirely feasible that any available punch could be used for hot-working. There is an example from the Mästermyr hoard of a lock-plate (find 116) with four square holes for the key tines, likely to have been made with a punch rather than stamped with a cold drill.[130] The

---

[125] Ottaway, 1992
[126] Hinton, 2000
[127] Ottaway, 1992
[128] Tipper & Dickens, 1992
[129] Hirst & Clark, 2009
[130] Arwiddson & Berg, 1983

other notable punch is find 12 from the smith's grave at Tattershall Thorpe (Lincolnshire) which appears to be a half-round and to have been used as a repoussé or stamping mark. Examples of punches from graves are rare (as are all tools) but they do exist: there is a pair recovered from grave 923 at Mucking II cemetery[131] datable to the 5th-7th centuries, along with two "tanged punches" likely to be graver's tools. The Mucking grave is of low status and indeterminate sex, based on the finds.

Tanged Punches

The name 'tanged punches' is something of a misnomer covering any punch- or chisel-like implement that tapers at both ends and is thicker in the middle, often with a step. The term is sometimes used by archaeologists as a coverall for any awl-like tool that defies immediate classification, since such tools can be used in many professions. A 'tanged punch' has only one drawback in that it doesn't work as a punch at all. All the user will do when striking such a tool is force the tang further into the handle. My experiments indicate that a punching function can be ruled out as the tool is designed for hand use only. The class of items now called 'tanged punches' will probably include a combination of graving tools, awls, picks, scribes and gouges in use by virtually every kind of craftsman including woodworkers, metalworkers, weavers and leatherworkers. Awls are discussed below in the section on leatherworking (p.91) in greater detail, but it must be noted that making a determination of function for such tools is impossible. 'Tanged punch' finds are widespread, as are awls. The designs are interchangeable and making distinctions between the two classes is largely subjective.

'Tanged punches' have been recovered from Coppergate (York), a total of 17 finds, the most unusual of which is no. 2244.[132] It is nominally 10mm in diameter and 10mm deep with a tang 24 mm long protruding from the back, apparently designed to be held in a wooden handle and presenting a flat round face for use. Its exact function is unknown but it is possible that it is some type of non-ferrous shaping tool. From Tattershall Thorpe (Lincolnshire) comes a burin (find 17) with a small wooden handle, no longer than 32mm which could be used as a scribe or hand awl.[133] The occupation deposits at Flixborough (Lincolnshire) gives us a tool which is presumed to be a mandrel due to its size, although in form it resembles a 'tanged punch'. It is find no. 3091[134] at 160mm long with equal lengths of tang and mandrel, 16mm in diameter tapering to a blunt point over 60mm or so, and designed for a handle. It would fit the physical requirements for a socket-making mandrel for ferrous metalworking. Lastly, from the Anglo-Saxon cemetery at Mucking II, (grave 923) come two small 'tanged punches' that in all likelihood are really awls.[135] 'Tanged punches' must therefore be viewed as a useful archaeological classification group rather than a separate tool type.

---

[131] Hirst & Clark, 2009
[132] Ottaway, 1992
[133] Hinton, 2000
[134] Evans & Loveluck, 2009
[135] Hirst & Clark, 2009

4 Tool Finds by Occupation

Nail Irons and Draw-Plates

Nail irons and draw-plates are an indispensable class of tool for the smith. The problem for modern researchers lies in distinguishing between the two archaeologically as their designs are essentially the same, and it is possible that some finds were used for both purposes.

In essence the nail iron is a rectangular bar with a tapering or rounded handle with a series of tapered holes punched though it for forming the nail ,which is forged with a square taper to correspond to the round taper of the nail iron. The nail blank is placed in the hole hot and the head formed by beating, then the nail iron is flipped over and the finished nail is tapped out as the tapered hole allows for its easy ejection.

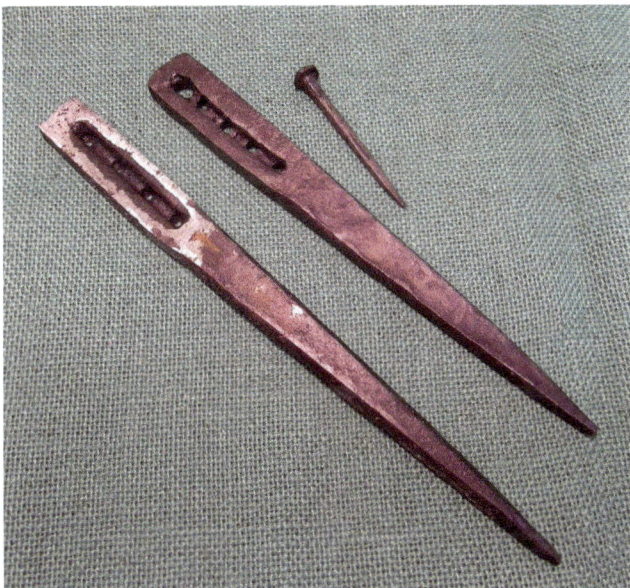

Figure 19 Reproductions (left:) Nail iron from Bygland, Norway. (right) Nail iron and nail from Tattershall Thorpe, Lincolnshire

There are two known nail iron draw-plate finds from Britain, both of which have Continental parallels. The first is the find from the smith's grave at Tattershall Thorpe[136] (Lincolnshire) of small dimensions, being only 114 mm long with a section at the head (work end) of 14x6mm tapering to a blunt point at the presumed handle end. The head is burred over from being struck, which would imply that it was hammered into a stock, post or tree, or possibly into a handle for hand-held use. It has five holes of varying sizes from the head end to the point (in order of 6, 4, 3, 1, 4 mm in diameter) and the iron has a slot in the reverse onto which the holes open. The 6 mm hole is larger than the slot and appears newer than the other (original?)

---

[136] Hinton,2000

holes so it may be an alteration for some specific task. Given the size of the smaller holes and the slot, this is likely to be a draw-plate. The burring to the head is from the smith's knocking the iron into a stock in order to steady it during non-ferrous metal drawing. The larger (6 mm) hole is probably a nail iron hole. There is a Scandinavian find of similar design from the smith's grave at Bygland (Norway) also with a slotted back.[137] This item is also likely to be a draw-plate.

The second find from Britain comes from the occupation site at Bloodmoor Hill, Carlton Coleville (Norfolk) (find no. 282); it is 166 mm long with a section of 21x17 mm, punched with four holes of similar sizes (from the head end 4.5, 5.6, 5 and 5.5 mm).[138] This tool again has a tapered handle and burred head from hammering into a block or handle. Given the uniformity of hole size and the dimensions of the cross-section, the tool is likely to be a nail-making iron as drawing wire to this thickness would be difficult. There is a parallel find in the Mästermyr hoard (find 86) of similar construction.[139] Both the Mästermyr and the Carlton Coleville nail irons have unslotted backs, with the hole-size making them unsuitable for drawing wire.

Pritchels

Pritchels are specialist hot-punches designed to be held at a distance (usually on a wooden arm) and used to make a shaped, punched hole in hot sheet. Four possible examples are known to exist. One pritchel from Thetford (Norfolk)[140] is 20 mm in diameter and around 100 mm long,; it is waisted at both ends, with an extra shaped reduction at the punch tip. This design may also facilitate the formation of a countersink - for instance, in the manufacture of horse shoes. A second find, also from Thetford, is a countersinking pritchel with a marked square-section step.[141] The pritchel is around 100 mm long with an off-centre punched 'eye' to accept a separate handle. There are references to a further two pritchels, one from Westley Waterless (Cambridgeshire)[142] and the other from Pakenham (Suffolk).[143]

---

[137] Blindheim, 1963
[138] Lucy, Tipper & Dickens, 2009
[139] Arwiddson & Berg, 1983
[140] Wilson, 1976
[141] Ottaway, n.d.
[142] Fox, 1923
[143] Wilson, 1976

4 Tool Finds by Occupation

Figure 20 Reproductions of the two Thetford pritchels

Blacksmiths' Clips

Blacksmiths' clips are a simple type of tool, formed as a pair of 'tweezers' with the arm permanently closed. The work piece is "clipped" into the end for further (usually hot-) working. Two such metalworking clips are known from the archaeological record. One is from the tool-set in the smith's grave at Tattershall Thorpe (find 6), nominally 300 mm long and 15mm wide tapering to around 5mm.[144] The clip is in two pieces, held together with two rivets. The second example comes from the occupation area at Bloodmoor Hill, Carlton Coleville (Norfolk) dated to the 6th - 8th centuries, (find no. 289);[145] it is much smaller than the Tattershall find, being only 115 mm long and 10 mm wide, parallel-sided and folded. Clips are rare additions to a smith's tool kit as far as surviving finds indicate, but they are very useful in holding material for further working.

---

[144] Hinton, 2000
[145] Lucy, Tipper & Dickens, 2009

4 Tool Finds by Occupation

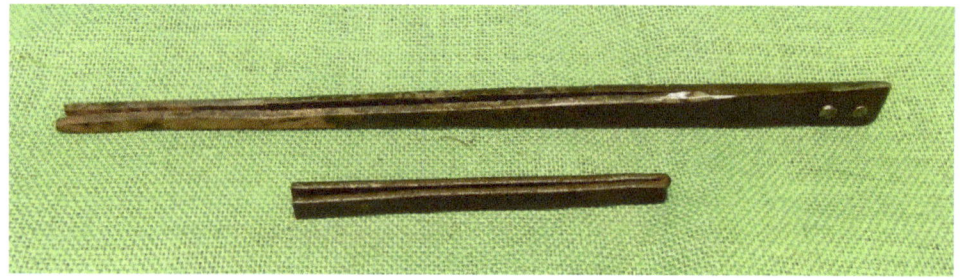

Figure 21 Reproduction metalworking clips.
(above) Tattershall Thorpe (below) Carlton Coleville

Soldering Boats

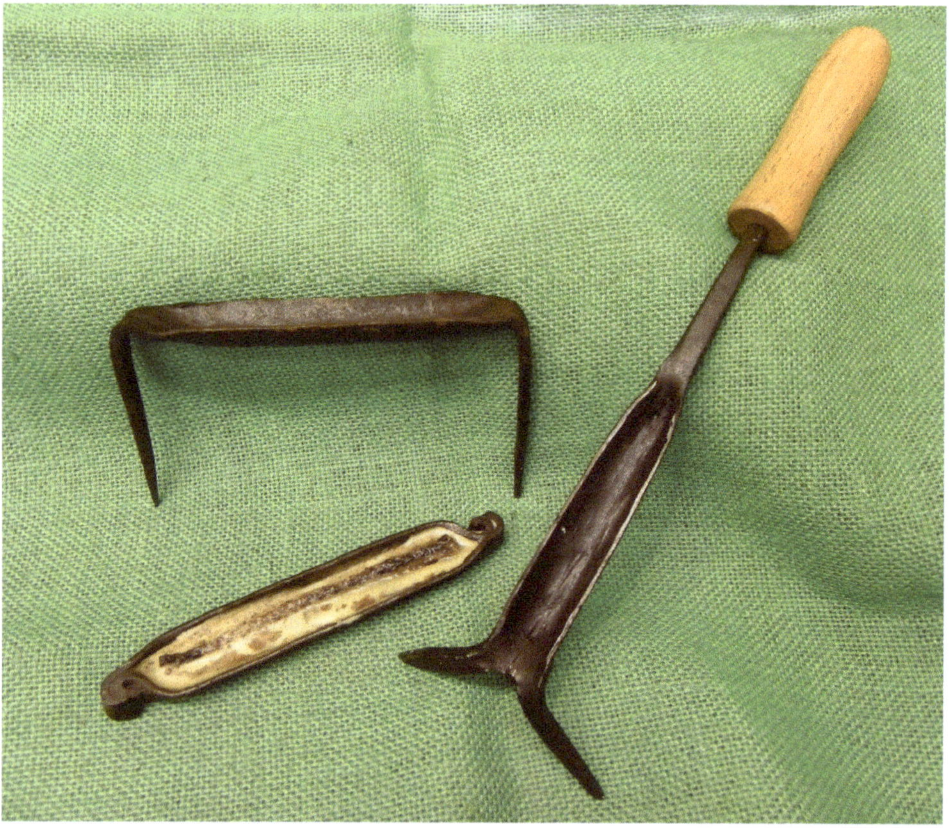

Figure 22 Soldering boats.
(left top) Mästermyr hoard; (left bottom) Coppergate, York (right) Tattershall Thorpe

Soldering boats are used as a heat-source in the soldering of non-ferrous metals. The known possible finds are badly corroded or fragmentary, making identification difficult. The soldering boat was filled with a tallow-soaked wick, then lit and the flame brought to bear underneath the workpiece producing sufficient heat to melt the lead-tin alloy solder.

As yet there has not been an identifiable find of a soldering iron from Britain. The only one known from a relevant context is from Illerup Ådal in Denmark.[146]

There is a possible soldering boat find from mid-Saxon London, from the Royal Opera House excavation (find M349, dated to 850-900AD), nominally 105 mm long and 17 mm in diameter (half round).[147] Unfortunately the find is fragmentary. From Coppergate (York) and dated to the mid-9th to late 10th century, come two possible boat fragments. No.2251 is 77 mm long and 17 mm wide, and no.2252 is 51 mm long and 12 mm wide. The absence of associated metalworking products or tools in the immediate vicinity of the finds does call this identification into question.

The find from the 7th c. smith's grave at Tattershall Thorpe does provide us with a complete, if damaged, find of a soldering boat some 85 mm long, tanged for a handle and with bifurcated feet providing steady support and a means for positioning the boat when in use.[148] Scandinavian finds of soldering boats from the Anglo-Saxon period can be found in a 12th century context at Lund (Sweden)[149], the Mästermyr hoard[150], and a similar find from Trelleborg (Sweden).[151]

Reamers

Reamers can be described as large, square-section awls designed for reaming out (enlarging) punched holes in iron and non-ferrous metals. It is entirely possible that some items identified as awls from metalworking sites are in fact small reamers. Only two definite examples of reamers are known, both from Lyminge (Kent) (finds 09.482 and 09.486).[152] Unfortunately no further information is available on these items as the work is at present only partly published.

Figure 23 Reconstructed reamer

---

[146] Dobat, 2008
[147] Malcolm, Bowsher & Cowie, 2003
[148] Hinton, 2000
[149] Mårtensson, 1976
[150] Arwiddson & Berg, 1983
[151] Nørlund, 1948
[152] Ottaway, 2012

4 Tool Finds by Occupation

Woodworking Tools

If there is one thing the Anglo-Saxons had in abundance, it was wood. Despite centuries of encroachment by agriculture, the woodland of Britain still stretched from coast to coast and the Anglo-Saxons were skilled at managing and working it! Here we shall review the evidence for woodworking tools.

Axes

The principal woodworking tool was the axe which had a number of forms according to the specifics of its function. Axes were often purely practical tools, but they also served as personal items. They are rare (but not unknown) burial finds which denotes some display of power or status for the user. These axes from inhumations in most cases are not for use on wood, but rather are designed for hewing flesh. Their inclusion in the grave is a personal statement: these axes were a weapon not destined for use in woodland clearance.

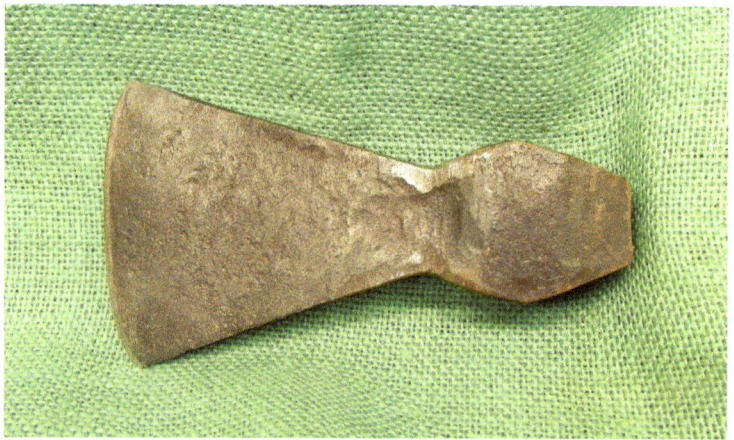

Figure 24 Reproduction of a Wheeler type 1 axehead

The commonest personal axe finds are *franciscas* - a light throwing-axe with a gracefully curved blade - or axe-hammers, such as the find from Mound 1 at Sutton Hoo, constructed from wrought iron (including its handle). It evidently held deep significance for its owner. However, all such finds are outside the subject of tools, and we concern ourselves here with axes for the cutting and working of wood.

In 1927, Wheeler put forward a classification of axeheads based on Anglo-Saxon and Viking finds with classes I to VI.[153] Within this formal classification are all the axehead types one is likely to encounter. There are only so many ways an axehead can be forged and each one is an individual item, so the classifications are rightly "loose" in application. Across the entire Anglo-Saxon period an evolution of axehead types can be seen, but dating them is difficult. For any individual axehead

---

[153] Wheeler, 1927

4 Tool Finds by Occupation

we can only generalise, because one manufactured in the 4th c. might still be in use during the 10th as the Nazeing hoard demonstrates.[154] Evidently, on that basis, some axes in use during the 14th and 15th centuries could have been manufactured prior to the Norman invasion.

Of the Wheeler classification axe-types, nos. 1 to 5 can be classed as having a tool function, while type 6 is the so-called 'Dane axe' which is a pure weapon type (and so will not be included for discussion).

Type 1

Find Spot Type 1 Axe	Dimensions mm Blade x length	Citation and remarks
Old London Bridge	50 x 175	Wheeler, 1927 fig 1/8
Putney (London)	75 x 175	Wheeler, 1927 fig 8/1
Walthamstow (Essex)	50 x 150	Wheeler, 1927 fig 8/2
Hurbuck hoard	60 x 190	Hodges, 1905; Wilson, 1968
Nazeing hoard	56 x 145	Morris axe no 1
Nazeing hoard	51 x 189	Morris axe no 2
Nazeing hoard	73 x 117	Morris axe no 4
Flixborough	85 x 160	Evans & Loveluck, 2009 Find 2423
Flixborough	57 x 185	Evans & Loveluck, 2009 Find 2452
Newmarket (Devils Dyke)	60 x 125	Fox, 1923

Type 2

Find Spot Type 2 Axe	Dimensions mm Blade x Length	Citation and remarks
River Thames, Brentwood	300 x 175	Wheeler, 1927 fig ¼, 9th C
River Thames, London	250 x 225	Wheeler, 1927 fig 1/5, 9th C
River Thames, London	200 x 125	Wheeler, 1927 fig 1/6, 9th C
Walthamstow	200 x 125	Wheeler, 1927 fig 1/1, 9th C
Crayke hoard	300 x 250	Wilson, 1976 no 1
Hurbuck hoard	120 x 190	Hodges, 1905; Wilson, 1968
Crayke Hoard	----------------	Wilson, 1976 fragmentary? no2
Winchester	350 x 200	Ottawa, n.d.
Milk Street, London	300 x 160	Vince, 1991 (Partial reconstructed blade)
Scraptoft Hoard	250 x 160	Leahy, 2012
Flixborough	195 x 170	Evans & loveluck, 2009, find 2455
Flixborough	200 x 160	Evans & Loveuck, 2009, find 2456
Flixborough	145 x 180	Evans & Loveluck, 2009 find 2453
Flixborough	160 x 140	Evans & Loveluck, 2009 find 2454
Tuddenham	75 x 90	Fox, 1923
Hauxton Cemetery	225 x 130	Fox, 1923

---

[154] Morris, 1983

4 Tool Finds by Occupation

Figure 25
Reproduction of a Wheeler type 2 axehead

Figure 26
Reproduction of a Wheeler type 3 axehead

The type 1 axe is considered to be light woodworking axe. Of note here is axe no.1 from the Nazeing hoard: according to Morris it is of a type in use from the Roman period in Britain and is possibly of Romano-British origin.[155] Against this assumption is the fact that this axe-type is of simple and effective design, so need not have altered much from the pre-Roman Iron Age. The sizes of axes of type 1 are consistent in blade-width to axehead length. They are for general woodworking use, including felling and splitting.

Wheeler type 2 axeheads are T-shaped, which is to say that from the socket a thin metal shaft terminates in a long thin blade at a right angle to the shaft. This is a pure woodworking tool designed for finishing planking by the light removal of wood across abroad front. Some of these axes are 'sided' which means that the cutting edges of the blades are ground in such a way as to give a shallow cutting angle on one side sloping to a flat edge on the opposite side.

---

[155] Morris, 1983

4 Tool Finds by Occupation

A peculiarity of the extant T-shaped axes is that the socket is centralised on the shaft which, for a sided tool, is a superficially unusual arrangement. More usually the blade would be offset to keep the axe as flat as possible against the workpiece, but keeping the socket centrally located allows the axe head to be removed and turned round on the shaft so it can be used as both a left- and right-handed axe. This practice avoids the need for two separate axeheads. Fortunately an axehead is known, designed with this function in mind, from the Anglo-Norman deposits in London at Milk Street. The axehead has an iron wedge in the side of the socket to allow the easy removal of the shaft, which is still intact and is curved so that when in use the user's knuckles are not caught on the woodwork.

There are no extant Roman models for this type of axe, giving rise to the presumption that it is a purely Germanic or Scandinavian style of tool. Wheeler argues that this style of axe is based on a Frankish model which was in use from the 9th to the 14th century.[156] However, the evidence from Hauxton(Cambridgeshire) is a grave find excavated by Hughes in 1891: the information is limited but it appears to be from an early Anglo-Saxon pre-Christian grave which would suggest that a Germanic introduction of the tool to Britain is at least probable.

Fox put forward the theory that the T-shaped axe evolved through time with an elongation of both blade and shaft.[157] But the evidence adduced is not totally convincing, as a medieval T-shaped axe from the Marlowe car park excavation in Canterbury (find 801) shows a very short wide shaft.[158] In this case the axe is also sided for use by a right-handed man and it may be the case that a further evolution of the design (or an increase in the availability of iron) has allowed the true 'siding' of T-shaped axes to take place, superseding the need for a multipurpose axe.

The T-shaped axe design varies, presumably due to the personal tastes of the original manufacturers. Both finds from the Crayke hoard illustrate this point: the larger of the two axes (no.2) has a flared socket and slender shaft whereas no. 1 has just a folded socket and shaft of the same width. This axe is either fragmentary or has by design an offset blade, making it an unusual piece not dissimilar to later medieval types.

Types 3, 4 and 5
The final three axehead types of the Wheeler classification system have been grouped together because they are similar in design. The type 3 bearded axes give way to the type 5 through the intermediate type 4. All these types are characterised by having flared or pinched sockets with the blade splaying out to a curved cutting edge. These axes are the ones most likely to be found in inhumations as they have a military aspect to them, as well as potentially being a woodworking tool.

---

[156] Wheeler, 1927, 1935
[157] Fox, 1923
[158] Blockley et al, 1995, p.1085

4 Tool Finds by Occupation

Find Spot Type 3 Axe	Dimensions mm Blade x Length	Citation & Remarks
River Thames, Whitehall	--------------	Shetelig, 1940, V.IV
London, The Strand	75 x 125	Wheeler, 1927, fig 9/1
Ballinaby Scotland	50 x 145	Shetelig, 1940, V.II
Ballinaby, Scotland	90 x 140	Shetelig, 1940, V.II

Find spot Type 4 Axe	Dimensions mm Blade x length	Citation & Remarks
Thames Street, London	100 x 160	Wheeler, 1927, fig 10/1
Aldergate, London	100 x 160	Wheeler, 1927, fig 10/2
Near Tower of London	100 x 150	Wheeler. 1927, fig 10/3
York	108 x 145	Pearson et al, 1981, D14
Jubbergate, York	164 x 210	Pearson et al, 1981
Knoc-Y-Doonee, Isle of Man	125 x 190	Shetelig, 1940
Pitt Rivers Museum, Oxford	---------	Shetelig, 1940
Sarre, Kent	130 x 130	Wilson, 1976
Hurbuck Hoard	85 x 125	Hodges, 1905; Wilson 1968
Nazeing Hoard	110 x 170	Morris, 1983, find 3

Find Spot Type 5 Axe	Dimensions mm Blade X Length	Citation & Remarks
Kew Bridge, London	125 x 160	Wheeler, 1927, Fig 9/2
Repton	120 x 150	Shetelig, 1940, p14, fig 2
Kiloranbay, Uist	135 x 205	Shetelig, 1940
Tote, Skye	---------	Shetelig, 1940
Reay, Caithness	---------	Shetelig, 1940
Hesket in the Forest, Cumberland	? x 190	Shetelig, 1940

Adzes

The adze is a carpenter's chipping tool for trimming wood split by the axe. The blade is set at 90° to the angle of the shaft and, like the axe, has two variant forms - the standard adze and the T-shaped adze. The latter is constructed using the same method as the T-shaped axe but with the socket in the side-face of the head. A number of adzes exist – they are not as numerous as axes which are more versatile tools. The adze finds are from the Hurbuck hoard, Flixborough and Thetford (where two adzes have been found, but only one is listed here).

4 Tool Finds by Occupation

Find Spot Adze	Dimensions, mm Blade x length	Citation and remarks
Hurbuck hoard (9th - 10th c.)	25 x 200	Hodges,1905; Wilson,1968
Thetford (8th to late 9thC)	60 x 150	Goodall,1984
Flixborough (Find 2425)	44 x 170	Evans & Loveluck, 2009
Flixborough (Find 2458 8th to late 9th c)	80 x 180	Evans & Loveluck, 2009
Carlton Coleville (Adze-hammer 6th - 8th c.)	22 x 73	Lucy,Tipper & Dickens,2009

Find Spot T adze	Dimensions, mm Blade x Length	Citation and remarks
Hurbuck hoard	210 x 130	Hodges, 1905. Wilson, 1968
Flixborough (Find 2459)	206 x 146	Evans & Loveluck, 2009

Figure 27 Reproduction of the Flixborough T-shaped adze.

Of particular note is find 2425 from Flixborough that has three iron wedges still in the socket. Of the T-shaped adzes there are limited finds: only two are listed here, one from the Hurbuck hoard and the other from Flixborough. The sizes of the T-shaped adze seems consistent across the two sites, and may represent the standard woodworking form. An adze any larger might prove unwieldy and ineffective at wood removal. The Flixborough find 2459 is unstratified but the styling is comparable to the datable axeheads at Flixborough and the similar design to the example in the Hurbuck hoard, which would suggest a date around the 9th century.

4 Tool Finds by Occupation

An adze not listed here is the fragmentary find from grave 145 in the Anglo-Saxon cemetery at Dover Buckland found broken and wedged in the grave cut – it is possible that it was broken during the digging of the chalk to form the grave.[159] The adze-hammer from the occupation deposits at Bloodmoor Hill (Norfolk) has been included amongst the adzes, but its construction with a small hammer head (8 mm diameter) to the reverse and very small socket (around 5 mm in diameter) is suggestive of a now missing iron handle. This may imply a mason's tool, although this is speculative, but from the same site find 336 is identified as a mason's pick which suggests some stone working among the community.

Spoon Augers

Spoon augers or spoon bits were the principal hole-drilling tool of the Anglo-Saxon period. There is effectively no limit to the size of hole that can be made with this type of tool: the head is bullet-shaped coming to a point, half-round with two cutting edges so that it can be used in either a clockwise or anticlockwise direction. It could be described as working like an inside-out pencil sharpener. The blade is straight with no twist and the socket end is usually flattened for fitting into a cross bar. Reproductions of finds have shown that this type of tool will work down to sizes as small as 5 mm wide. A number of sites have produced spoon augers of varying sizes, attesting to their importance in various wood-utilisation processes with a presumed primary use in the building and shipbuilding industries.

Find Spot	Date	Find Ref.	Tip width and remarks
Hurbuck hoard	9th c.	----	Complete auger
Fishergate, York	Early 8th c.	4942	5mm
Fishergate, York	8th - 9th c.	4944	12mm
Fishergate, York	Late 8th c.	4943	fragmentary
Fishergate, York	Mid 11th c.	4945	fragmentary
Coppergate, York	9th -11th c.	2260	Fragmentary shaft
Coppergate, York	9th -11th c.	2261	Fragmentary shaft
Coppergate, York	9th -11th c.	2262	25mm complete auger
Coppergate, York	9th -11th c.	2263	Fragmentary tip
Coppergate, York	9th -11th c.	2264	13mm complete auger
Coppergate, York	9th -11th c.	2265	Fragmentary tip
Coppergate, York	9th -11th c.	2266	13mm complete auger
Coppergate, York	9th -11th c.	2268	Fragmentary auger
Flixborough	?	2462	32mm Unstratified find
Flixborough	?	2463	24mm Unstratified find
Flixborough	?	2464	30mm Unstratified find
Royal Opera House London[160]	675-730AD	M24	20mm wide tip 285mm Long

---

[159] Evison, 1987
[160] Malcolm, Bowsher & Cowie, 2003

4 Tool Finds by Occupation

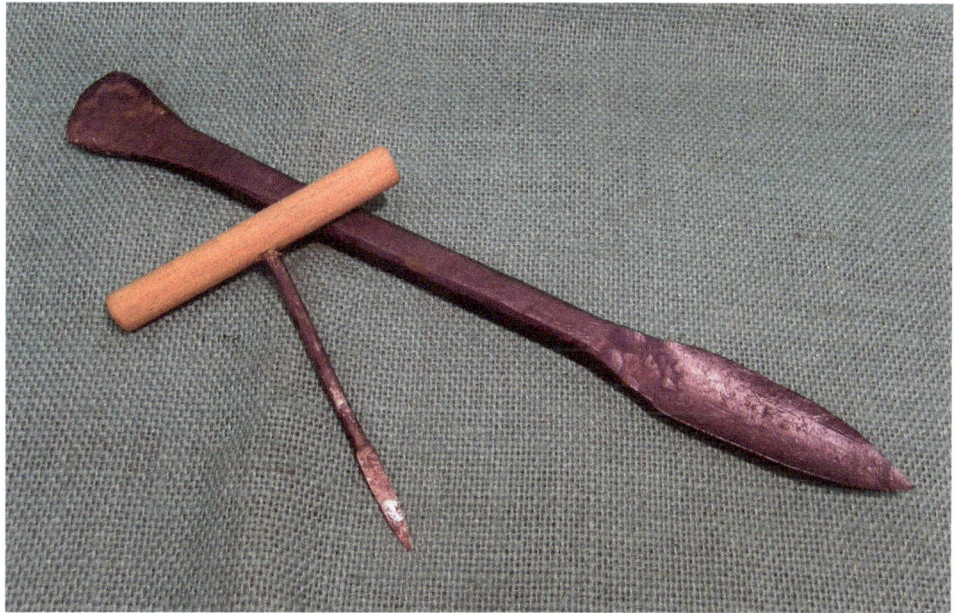

Figure 28 Reproduction spoon augers, 25 mm and 5 mm

The spoon augers from Flixborough have been included here (even though they are unstratified finds) as they are likely to be of Anglo-Saxon origin.[161] According to Manning the spoon auger has remained unchanged since the Roman period and in fact the design is so good that it is still in use today.[162] Most surviving spoon augers are of the larger diameters for the boring of heavy timbers, but smaller finds do exist, such as the example from Fishergate, York (4942). There is a small auger from 21-33 Aldwark, York[163] and another from Thetford[164] all comparable in size to the Coppergate find (no.2268). Also from Thetford are a further three small spoon augers from the 10th century levels. In Britain there are further finds from the 11th century deposits at Goltho[165] (Lincolnshire) and at Westley Waterless (Cambridgeshire),[166] from Cheddar[167] (Somerset) and Skerne[168] (North Humberside). And finally, two nearly complete examples were found in *Lundenwic* (London) in an 8th c. context at 2-26 Shorts Gardens.

---

[161] Evans & Loveluck, 2009
[162] Manning, 1985
[163] MacGregor, 1978
[164] Goodall, 1984
[165] Goodall, 1987
[166] Fox, 1923
[167] Goodall, 1979
[168] Dent, 1984

Spoon auger finds from further afield are well documented, such as the six finds from the Mästermyr hoard[169] ranging in size from 19 mm down to 7 mm.

Analysis of the spoon auger finds from Coppergate[170] shows that at least two of them were used in a clockwise cutting direction, evidenced by the wear pattern on the tip of find 2265 and the twist in the shaft of 2266.

Breast Augers

The use of the breast auger at this time is presumed, and there is a clear depiction of one in use on the Bayeux Tapestry.[171] From my own experimentation, the breast auger does have a better cutting rate especially on the larger auger sizes. Further experimentation has shown that on the smaller augers (under 10 mm) a handle in line with the shaft is quite sufficient for twisting the auger: any larger than this and a flat T-shaped bar (the handle set at 90° to the shaft) is required for two-handed twisting of the blade. This effect is clearly illustrated in the larger spoon augers, as the shaft has a flattened, spatulate tang for fitting into the crossbar slot.

Chisels and Gouges

Chisels and gouges are cutting tools employed in the secondary working of wood. They are designated as having a cutting edge and either a tanged or socketed wooden handle designed to be used either by hand or with a mallet. Hand gouges, being smaller and requiring little force to use them, are usually tanged and it seems that only the larger chisels were socketed; the smaller chisels were also tanged. Since finds are usually without evidence for their handles we cannot say if they ever had ferrules to stop the handle splitting. Chisels and gouges have been grouped together here as a matter of convenience.

Figure 29

Reproduction chisel from the Crayke hoard

---

[169] Arwiddson & Berg, 1983
[170] Ottaway, 1992
[171] Stenton, 1957, fig 38

4 Tool Finds by Occupation

Find Spot	Find Reference	Remarks and dimensions, mm
Brandon, Suffolk[172]	------	Presumed turner's chisel, Middle Saxon context 150 mm long
Coppergate, York	2269	U section gouge 10mm wide, x 100mm long, dogleg
Coppergate, York	2270	V section Gouge, 8mm wide, x 80mm long
Nazeing hoard	14	One piece iron gouge 140mm long x 17mm gouge tip, curved
Carlton Coleville[173]	321	Paring chisel 87 long x 19mm wide
Carlton Coleville	322	Paring chisel 130mm long x 23mm wide
Carlton Coleville	323	Paring chisel 29mm long x 17mm wide
Carlton Coleville	326	Chisel fragment
Carlton Coleville	327	Possible mortice chisel, one piece, 113mm long x 12mm wide
Carlton Coleville	330	Socketed chisel/gouge 81mm long x 18mm wide
Crayke Hoard	----	Socketed chisel, 9th-10thC, 150mm long x 15mm wide
Flixborough	2426	Unstratified find, likely to be Anglo-Saxon, 145mm long x 55mm wide

The finds from Carlton Coleville (Norfolk) are dated 6th to the 8th c. and are from the occupation deposits; the mortice chisel (no.327) is a one-piece iron chisel and like the one-piece find (no.14) from the Nazeing hoard it would have been struck with a hammer rather than a mallet (the burring on the Nazeing example attests to this). These examples could also be metalworking chisels as the tip profile cannot be ascertained in current preservation. The turner's chisel from Brandon (Suffolk) has a cup between tang and shaft not dissimilar to modern examples, and the tang is bent at around 45°, which may have been intentional to produce an angled chisel (if not accidental damage after use). The Coppergate examples are dated to the 9-10th century.

Shaves

Shaves encompass a number of variant forms. Included here are curved shaves (sometimes referred to as bowl shaves, although there is little evidence they were used in bowl manufacture), spoke shaves and draw knives. With curved shaves the handle form is difficult to ascertain, and either of two forms is likely - a crossbar linking the two arms of the shave onto a common shaft, or a handle for each individual end. With the smaller types of curved shave the linked handle seems appropriate. My own experiments have shown the larger shaves working well with individual handles.

---

[172] Ottaway, n.d.
[173] Lucy, Tipper & Dickens, 2009

Curved or Bowl Shaves

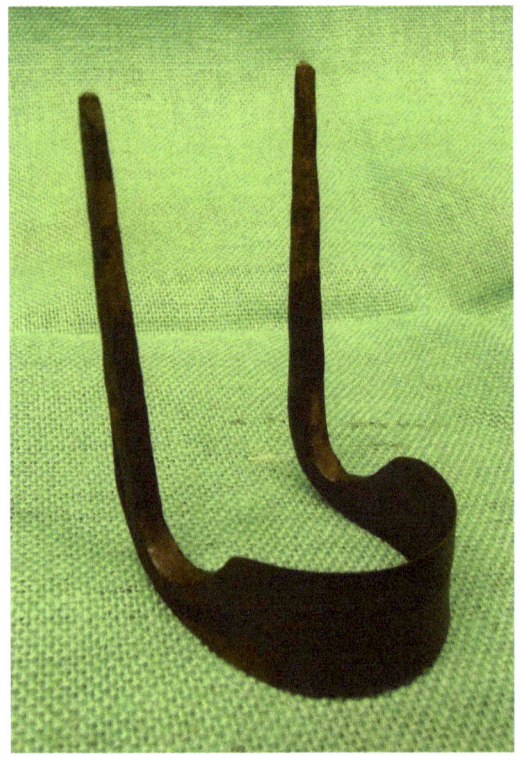

Curved shaves are a rare find in occupation deposits, and only four complete examples are available for investigation - two of which (both from Flixborough, Lincolnshirw) are unstratified but likely to be of Anglo-Saxon origin and date. The Coppergate shave is unusual in that the blade is set at 90° to the handle which, on reconstructions I have made, renders the shave difficult to use. It is possible that this example was constructed with a specific function in mind. All the other curved shaves are set at 45° and experiments have shown that they work well for grooving flat wood.

Figure 30 Reproduction of Coppergate shave 2259

Find Spot Curved Shaves	Find Number	Date	Remarks
Coppergate, York	2259	$9^{th}\ 11^{th}$ c.	70mm wide set 90°
Flixborough	2460	?	160mm wide set 45°
Flixborough	2461	?	122mm wide set 45°
Carlton Coleville	333	6th-8th c.	94mm wide set 45°

Draw Knives

A draw knife is a flat blade with a tanged handle at either end, set at either 90° or 45° to the blade. No complete examples are known, but fragmentary finds do exist exhibiting both types of tang angle. There is an unusual type found at Coppergate (York, no. 2984) which is fragmentary but comprises half a blade and a curled tang. The size of the curl suggests an easy fit for the thumb, so the piece could be described as a "thumb shave". Experiments with a replica have shown that it is a versatile and useful shaving tool with a number of applications, one advantage being that it fits easily into a pouch. There is a similar example from the Lough Gur Crannog, Co. Limerick, Ireland, likely to be of the same design type.[174]

---

[174] O Riordain, 1994

4 Tool Finds by Occupation

Figure 31 Reproduction of the Coppergate thumb shave

Examples of the more standard drawknife design include a fragmentary find also from Coppergate (number 2988) with a deformed 45° tang. From Sandton in Kent comes a fragmentary 90°-tanged drawknife (British Museum accession number 1950,1002.88) of 102 mm extant length.[175] A find from the occupation deposits at Bishopstone in East Sussex (find no. 44) with one tang intact at 90° to the blade which is 117mm long.[176] All these drawknives are small, indicating use on semi-finished wood of small size, although it could equally be said that the Bishopstone drawknife could be a small reaping hook.

My own reconstructions of these small drawknives have given good results on wood of small section. It could be argued that these small shaves negate the need for woodworking planes, which are more difficult to use. Finally there is a drawknife fragment from the Marlowe car park excavation in Canterbury (find no. 762), almost complete at 22cm long, dated to the Anglo-Saxon period still with a tang intact.[177]

---

[175] Wilson, 1968
[176] Thomas, 2010
[177] Blockley et al, 1995

4 Tool Finds by Occupation

Figure 32 reproduction of a drawknife from Coppergate, York (find 2988)

Spoke Shaves

Spoke shave finds are more numerous than drawknife finds, they use less metal than an equivalent sized drawknife and the spread of these items around Britain may suggest they were the preferred shaving tool. Many of the spoke shave finds are classed as drawknife blades due to their pierced terminals, in line with the theory that the handles were "loose" or poorly secured to the blade. This theory is unlikely to be valid as reconstructions have shown that the user has little control over the blade and, if unlucky, may lose a finger!

The construction of this shaving tool is simple - a basic triangulate knife blade of the same width throughout its length with each end pierced to take a fixing peg or nail. The handle is likely to have been constructed as in modern examples - a long wooden bar with the blade secured in the middle by the nails and a rebate in the handle to allow the shavings an easy means of escape.

Figure 33 Reproduction of the Sutton Courtenay spoke shave

4 Tool Finds by Occupation

Figure 34 An alternative interpretation of the blade mounting

Alternatively it is possible that the blade was fixed between two handles set at right angles to each other as shown in the reconstruction (fig.33). If properly constructed, the spoke shave can be set to take off differing thicknesses of wood. Reconstructions of this tool are easily used, requiring little skill (in a relative sense).

There is a possible alternative construction of the spoke shave set in a curved handle allowing the spoke shave to act like a drawknife: this construction is speculative but highly functional – fig 34.

The Bishopstone and Sutton Courtenay finds were from the occupation deposits and show a development in the use of the spoke shave from the early to late Anglo-Saxon periods. Further examples have been found at: Burrow Hill, Butley (Suffolk) - three finds in a Middle Anglo-Saxon context;[178] Riby (Lincolnshire);[179] Repton (Derbyshire)[180] two finds; and three more from Lyminge (Kent)[181] - finds 08.158, 08.159 and 09.265. Sizes for the Lyminge shaves are currently unavailable as the work is unpublished. As can be seen from the lengths of the surviving shaves, sizes vary from 70 mm to 200 mm indicating a wide range of woods and techniques.

Find spot Spoke shaves	Find number	Length mm	remarks
Flixborough	2448	205	unstratified
Flixborough	2449	145	Early to mid 9th c.
Coppergate	2982	110	9-10thC
Thwing[182]	7617?	130	---------
Bishopstone[183]	45	136	Late Anglo-Saxon
Sutton Courtenay[184]	1923.848	70	Early Anglo-Saxon

---

[178] Fenwick, 1984
[179] Ottaway, 1994
[180] Excavated by M. Biddle.
[181] Unpublished; cited in Ottaway, 2012
[182] Ottaway, 2012
[183] Thomas, 2010

Hammers and Mallets

Most hammers can be used for a multitude of striking functions. The only type of iron hammer with a presumed woodworking function is the claw hammer with a bifurcated tail for the removal of nails from woodwork. This does not necessarily imply that the strike-face was used for woodworking, it merely suggests a multi-purpose tool used for building.

From the Anglo-Saxon period in Britain there are three claw hammers currently known. Two are from the site at Goltho[185] (Lincolnshire), each around 4" (100 mm) in length and a third damaged example from Bishopstone[186] (Kent) of similar size. The Bishopstone hammer is clearly an adaptation of the standard period hammerhead with the tapering tail split to form the claw. One of the examples from Goltho is constructed in a modern style (albeit in a poorly forged form) with an unusual square socket and curved claws.[187]

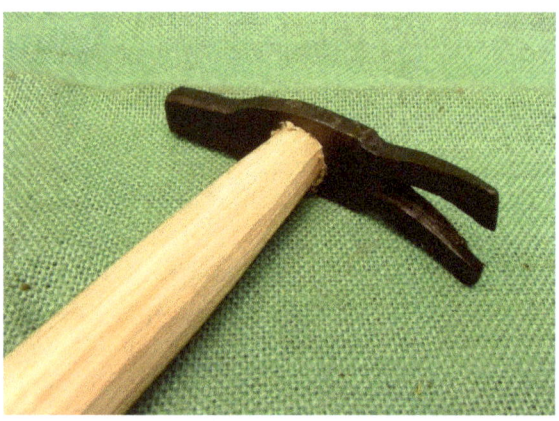

Figure 35 Reproduction of a Goltho-style claw hammer

It is worth noting that with my hammer reconstructions, the hammerhead pulls out of the shaft fairly easily when trying to remove nails. It is possible that the original Goltho style hammers had a steel-encased wooden shaft to increase the leverage. Late Viking and early medieval models from Novgorod (Russia) avoided this problem by having an all-steel head and shaft either brazed or peened on.[188] As yet there are no similar finds from the Anglo-Saxon period in Britain known to me.

Mallets are wooden hammers used in carpentry. Remarkably, a number of examples survive; from Anglo-Norman London dated to the late 11th or early 12th century.[189] Find 373 is the maplewood head of a mallet some 84 mm in diameter, from the Milk Lane site. A mallet (no. 8186) from Coppergate (York) is 100 mm in diameter and

---

[184] Leeds, 1923, Ashmolean collection AN1923.848
[185] Goodall, 1987
[186] Thomas, 2010
[187] Reproduced in Ottaway; n.d.
[188] Brisbane & Hather 2007
[189] Vince, 1991

made from willow with a hazel shaft.[190] Further examples from Coppergate include two mallets found in the 'A' deposit dated to the 10th c. with a further York mallet found in Clifford Street (and now in the Yorkshire Museum) with a rounded head and a V shaped tail - not dissimilar to modern silver- or pewtersmiths' hammers.[191] Moving further afield, a number of finds form Ireland add to our corpus of mallet heads:

Date Range	Find	Findspot	Published
6th - 9th c.	1	Ballinderry Crannog 2	Hencken, 1936
7th - 11th c.	2	Lagore Crannog	Hencken, 1950
10th -11th c.	1	Ballinderry Crannog 1	Hencken, 1936
11th c,	4	Viking Dublin	Morris, 1984

Bow Drills

According to Goodman[192] the only representations of Roman boring tools depict bow drills but after the Roman era the bow drill was little used by woodworkers who preferred the more powerful breast auger, of which none have been found in an Anglo-Saxon context (p.68ff). Experimental reconstructions of bow drills show they have limited applications in woodworking: the power of the drill is very low which limits the maximum size of drill head to about 4 mm maximum. This type of tool is mostly used in the drilling of bone and antler, where small holes are required.

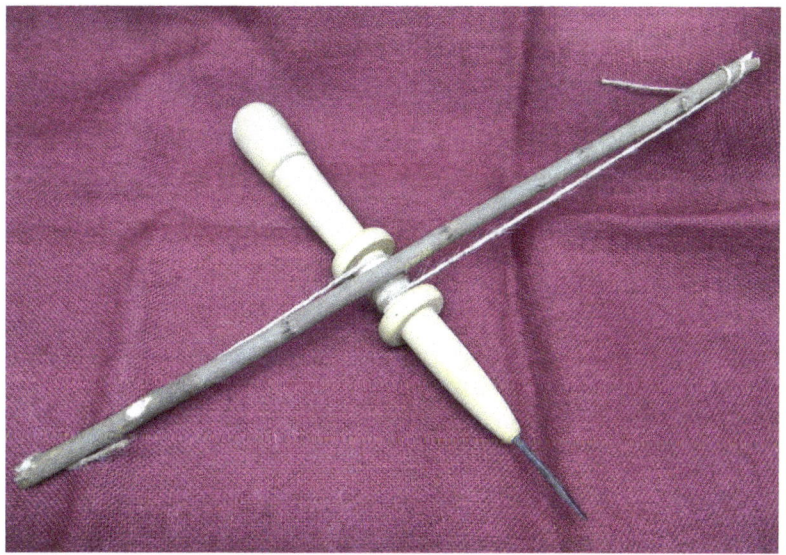

Figure 36 Reproduction 5mm bow drill

---

[190] Ottaway, 1992
[191] Benson, 1906
[192] Goodman, 1984

4 Tool Finds by Occupation

Gimlets & Borers

These are woodworking tools designed to bore holes. They are not dissimilar in function to spoon augers, but are of a simpler design. There are two gimlets known from York: the first is a fragmentary tip from Coppergate (find 2267) dated to the 9th - 11th century and the second is from Fishergate, a complete example (no. 494)7, 150 mm long with a spatulate head for fixing into a wooden crossbar. The gimlet has a tapering square section head twisted into a spiral, not dissimilar to a modern screw. Experimental reconstructions show that this type of tool is not very effective at giving a clean cut in wood and leaves a rough hole, but it is useful for creating a guide-hole for the spoon auger. It is therefore likely that this tool was used in conjunction with the auger.

The second type of drilling tool is the borer which is, in basic form, a flat drill without a twisted shaft and with a head angled at around 45°. There is an example in the Hurbuck hoard of a large borer with spatulate head for a crossbar,[193] and reconstructions show that it can produce a quick if somewhat rough hole in wood.

Figure 37 Reproduction auger from Coppergate, York (no.2267)

Wedges

Wedges are used to split wood for further working. They can be classified into two main categories - those made of iron and those of wood. Wooden wedges are considerably larger than iron wedges (wood is a lot cheaper than iron) and are usually constructed of oak which, when seasoned, is very hard. It is possible that some of the smaller examples are more likely to be hafting wedges (used to wedge the head of a tool onto its handle) as can be seen in extant examples from Flixborough (axe 2425) and the axe wedge from Milk Street, London (find no. 26). The assumption is that the iron wedges are for finer or seasoned wood splitting and the wooden versions for unseasoned green woodworking. However a need for fine wood splitters comparable in size to hafting wedges cannot be ruled out.

---

[193] Hodges,1905; Wilson,1968

4 Tool Finds by Occupation

Find spot Iron wedges	Date	Qty	Remarks and Citation
Bishopstone, Sussex	8th - 11th c.	6	Small wedges. Thomas, 2010
Flixborough, Lincolnshire	9th - 11th c.	18	8 unstratified. Evans & Loveluck, 2009
Sarre cemetery, Kent	6th c.	1	Grave 233. Wilson, 1968
Christchurch place, Dublin, Ireland	10th - 11th c.	3	Morris, 1984
St Aldates, Oxford	Mid 9th c.	1	Goodall, 1977
Stanton Chair, Suffolk	-----	2	Possible wedges. Morris, 1984
Winchester cathedral Green	1090-3 AD	3	Small wedges. Goodall, 1990
Coppergate, York	9th - 11th c.	1	Find 2257. Goodall, 1990. Ottaway, 1992

Find spot wooden wedges	Date	Qty	Remarks and Citation
Coppergate, York	9-11thC	13	All Oak. Morris, 2000
Pavement, York	9-11thc	3	MacGregor, 1982
Ballinderry Crannog 2 Ireland	6-9thC	?	Hencken, 1942
North Elmham	---	1	Wade-Martins, 1980
New Fresh Wharf London	11thC	1	Prichard & Morris, 1991

Find	Material	Long mm	Wide mm	Thick mm
2257	Iron	60	25	8
8175	oak	140	116	32
8178	oak	84	34	12
8179	oak	140	40	32
8184	oak	90	18	20
8185	oak	140	14	10
484	oak	115	22	16
485	oak	118	22	16
486	oak	155	78	55

Included above is a list of wedge sizes of the finds from York dated to the 9th to 11th centuries for comparison. As can be seen, the iron wedges are smaller than the wooden finds but there is a comparable oak find similar in size to the Coppergate iron wedge (Coppergate 8178). It is likely that wedges smaller than this were used, because the longevity of a small wooden wedge is unimportant as they can easily be replaced (York Pavement finds 484-486, all others are from Coppergate).

4 Tool Finds by Occupation

Figure 38 Reproduction iron (left) and wooden wedges

Lathes

As far as we can discern, the highest form of Anglo-Saxon tool mechanisation was the reciprocating lathe, more commonly known as the pole lathe, a device whose roots extend into prehistory with finds dated as far back as the late Iron Age site at Glastonbury lake village.[194]

Anglo-Saxon lathes have two basic forms: the pole lathe and the bow lathe. These are essentially similar devices except that the power to a pole lathe is provided by the operator whereas the bow lathe requires a separate worker to power it. The 'pole' is a length of springy timber to the upper end of which a cord is attached; the cord passes round the workpiece and down to a treadle. The operator presses down with his foot, causing the cord to be pulled downwards thus rotating the workpiece and pulling the end of the pole down; the tension in the pole is then released by freeing the treadle so that the cord is pulled upwards and the workpiece rotates in the opposite direction. The workpiece is held at either end by a pair of pivots on stocks which rotate freely, usually attached to a frame or bench.

No physical examples of lathes exist from the Anglo-Saxon period: being made of wood, were probably burnt once they were broken, or parts utilised for other purposes. The only metal components in a pole lathe would be the iron centres (pivot points) on the head stocks, and indeed one such fragment does exist - find 8237 from Coppergate (York), a wooden tool rest support dated to 975-mid 11th c.

---

[194] Bulleid & Gray, 1911, fig 67. Mechanisation in the making and playing of musical instruments was also very sophisticated.

The evidence for the pole lathe is extensive in their output, in both finished artefacts and their resultant waste, such as the wooden cores of lathe-turned bowls and cups. According to Morris:[195]

> *"Turning on a pole-lathe is a skill acquired gradually by experience, and a craft which had to be taught and learned if a living was to be based on it"*

My own limited attempts at pole lathing clearly show that this is so. It requires extensive hand-eye and foot coordination. As the lathe is a reciprocating tool powered by a vertically traversing strap that spins the workpiece first clockwise then anticlockwise, it can be difficult to work with. The most skilful workers, it is said, know how to not only work the bowl on the up and down strokes but also to multiple bowl cut, i.e. they can cut the inner face of one bowl on the down stroke and cut the outer of the core to form another bowl on the upstroke.

Figure 39 Reproduction of a bow lathe

The pole lathe was probably the most important tool in the manufacture of domestic tableware.[196] It was instrumental in producing a comparatively cheap and durable product required by every household.

From the Anglo-Saxon period there is no evidence (as yet) for the existence of a continuous rotary lathe. However there are a number of waterwheel sites[197] - at least

---

[195] Morris, 2000
[196] Morris, 2000
[197] Alexander, 2011

nine excavated dating from the 7th century onwards and another fifty in charter references - where the rotary grinding of corn took place, so they certainly had the capability of manufacturing such a lathe. Normally lathes are situated in the woodland near the point of felling rather than sited for proximity to a source of power.

Finds of pole lathe tools are rare but there is a notable find from York, made at the corner of Coppergate and Castlegate in 1906[198] (find no. 9183) of a socketed hook-ended chisel, the design of which is still in use today for woodturning. There is also a 9th c. socketed tool whose end curves round to form a hook, found at Portchester castle in a pit with two bow drills and four lathe-turned cores.[199]

The bow lathe works on the same principle as the pole lathe but its reciprocating power is provided by a bow whose string is wrapped round the power shaft. It requires the use of a co-worker to power the shaft and the operator to handle the cutting and shaping. This two-man team implies a more expensive form of tool in terms of man-hours. A leg (used on a pole lathe) is stronger than an arm (used on a bow lathe) so the size of object that can be attempted on a bow lathe would be considerably smaller than that made on a pole lathe. The bow lathe does allow the user more control over his work as he is freed from the exertion of powering the lathe. It is likely that finer products were manufactured on this type of tool, such as bone and antler shafting and finely-turned woodwork. In addition the bow lathe with a suitable collet can be made to turn amber, jet and shale, as some surviving drop spinning weights attest.

Planes

There is currently only one certain example of a woodworking plane find from Britain, from Sarre (Kent).[200] Construction of the plane is unusual as it is made of bone plaques with a copper-alloy sole plate and, according to Goodman, is roughly contemporary with Frisian examples dated to around 600 AD.[201] The plane is 13.5 cm long, 30 mm wide and 30 mm high with a 20 mm wide iron blade set at 43°. Goodman's wooden reconstruction was; *"remarkably easy to use although setting of the iron was a little tricky"* which reflects problems encountered with modern reconstructions. The limitation with this type of planes is that it cannot take off large amounts of material as one does with a modern plane, but is mainly used for finishing work. The plane's blade has a tendency to jump out of the socket if overworked.

Originally the Sarre plane was catalogued as a lock, so unusual was the find, but a re-appraisal determined its true function. It is rather well made with the sole plate secured by three iron rivets and teardrop-shaped washers - a decorative flourish unusual on any Anglo-Saxon tool. Given the age of the plane and its style, it is possible that it is either a Roman plane re-used or a local copy of a Roman design.

---

[198] Benson, 1906, p. 73, pl ii
[199] Cunliffe, 1976
[200] Dunning, 1959
[201] Goodman, 1965, ref.44

As the fine drawknife from Bishopstone (Sussex) implies, there may have been little requirement for a plane in the Anglo-Saxon workshop with the drawknife taking over this function. Experiments have shown that, in skilled hands, the drawknife is a very effective wood finishing tool.

Figure 40 Reproduction small ashwood plane

Leatherworking Tools

Leatherworking tools have limited if not unique forms which are readily identifiable in the archaeological record. The main extant metal leatherworking and tanning tool is the slicker. There is no evidence for the use of curriers knives (knives with a pronounced S-shaped blade produced by wear) in an Anglo-Saxon context: these knives first appear during the Anglo-Norman period from the 12th century onwards and were used to de-flesh and scrape the leather during the tanning process. It is likely that the slicker had a similar function.

Slickers

The slicker (or sleaker) is a flat-bladed knife with a tang at both ends set at 90° to the blade, to which the handles are attached. On first appearances it looks not dissimilar to a draw knife, but with the edge of the blade on the outer face. The function of the slicker is to force out the dirt from under the hair roots below the grain layer, and to shave the flesh side to produce a leather of consistent thickness.[202]

Slicker finds are fairly well distributed around Britain, attesting to the widespread manufacturing of leather. There is an example of the Middle Anglo-Saxon period from Hamwic (Southampton) (find no; SOU169.2572)[203] and some later Anglo-Saxon

---

[202] Goodall, 1990
[203] Southampton City Council, unpublished

finds from Beverley (Yorkshire)[204], Winchester (Hampshire)[205] and Flixborough (Lincolnshire)[206] all dated to the early to the 9th c, There are four finds in total from Flixborough (find nos. 2471 to 247)4 with 2473 being the only intact example from that site. Both the Flixborough and Winchester finds are of roughly equal size at 150 mm long implying that this was a customary standard size. Finally, a complete slicker from the Marlowe car park excavation in Canterbury (Kent) is also 150 mm in length.[207]

Figure 41 Reproduction of the Winchester slicker

Lunettes

As regards tools for working finished leather, the finds are even more restricted with only one leatherworking lunette from Flixborough (Lincolnshire) (find 2475) dating from the mid to late 9th c. This tool consists of a crescent-shaped blade with a handle set centrally at 90° to the edge; it is an effective leather cutting tool still used today. There is a similar find from Portmahomack, Moray Firth, Scotland from a Pictish monastic site which would suggest that this type of tool was known and used widely across Britain.[208]

---

[204] Goodall, 1991
[205] Goodman, 1990
[206] Evans & Loveluck, 2009
[207] Blockley et al, 1995
[208] Carver, 2004

4 Tool Finds by Occupation

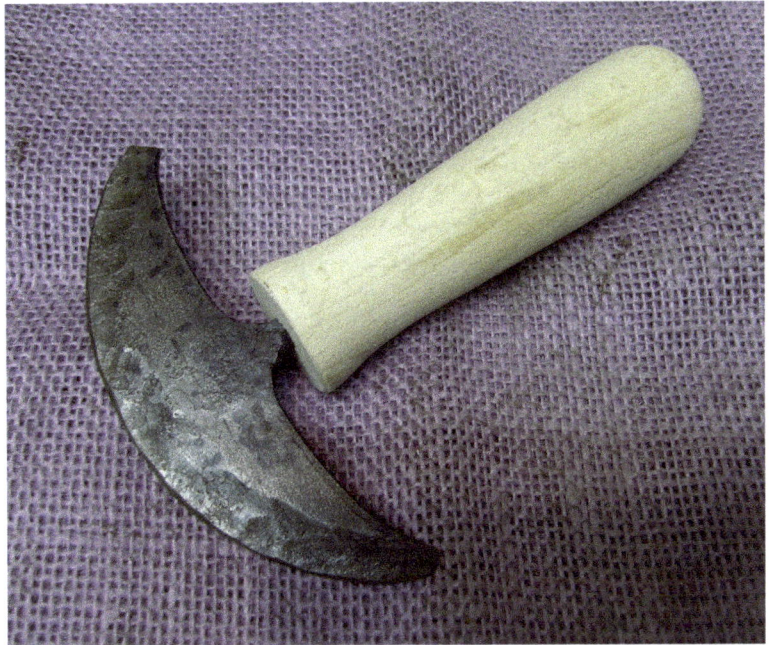

Figure 42 Reproduction of the Fixborough lunette

Shears

In the cutting of leather, most small knives will serve well and there is no reason that shears could not have been used in leather-cutting. Experiments show that shears used for cutting leather do need a stronger spring arm. which would be reflected in the strength required by the user. Shears from presumed leatherworking sites can therefore be viewed as having a leatherworking function.

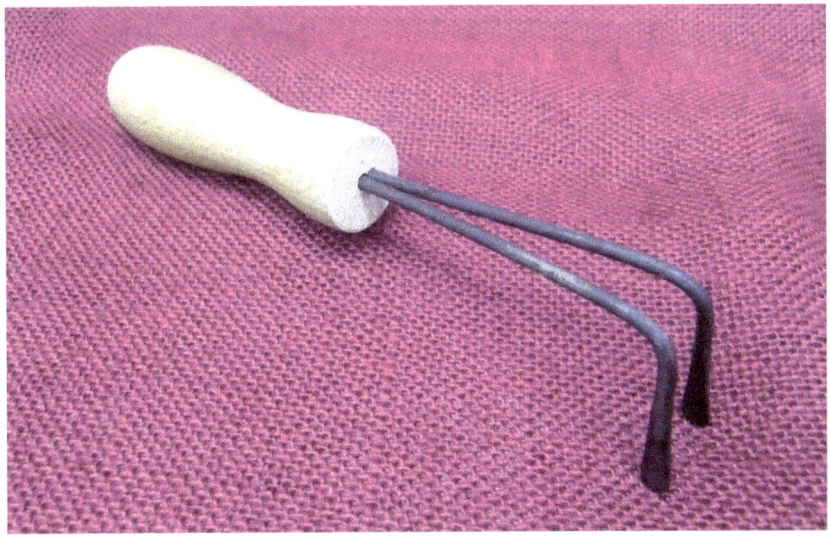

Figure 43 Reproduction of a leatherworker's creaser

4 Tool Finds by Occupation

Creasers
From Coppergate (York) and dated to the 9th c. come four finds of leatherworkers' creasers (finds 2744-47). [209] Each is a two-armed device, the arms bent at 90° at the end and set in a wooden handle. The distance between the arms is set by pulling the arms apart. The tool is used to form a decorative straight line (and guide for stitching) along the edge of leather. Used hot on damp leather to singe the line in and seal the end fibres of the cut leather, this tool has changed little in two thousand years with its modern counterpart differing only in having the arms set by screw thread.

Tanning Tool
A tool with a probable Anglo-Saxon context comes from the Cemetery II area (a Roman ditch) at Mucking (Essex) with a possible date of the 5th to 8th c.[210] It is nevertheless possible that this may be a Roman period residual (casual loss?) item. The tool (number 21) consists of a flat, D-shaped blunt serrated blade around 50 mm wide with a socket to the rear; it may have been used in the primary working of skins during the tanning process.

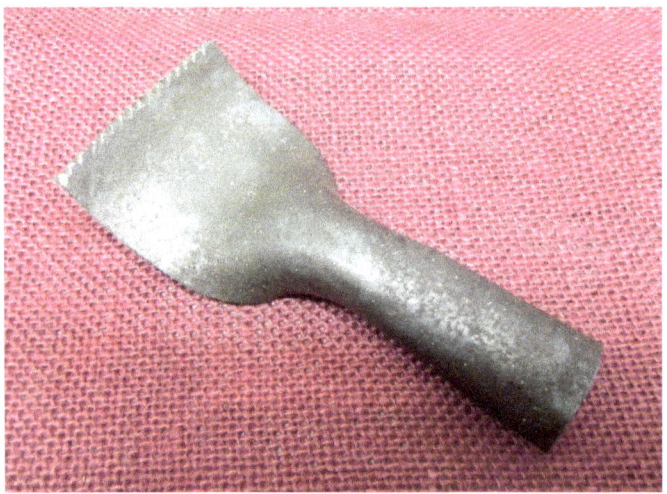

Figure 44 Reproduction tanning (?) tool from Mucking

Shoe Lasts
Surviving wooden tools are rare finds but fortunately from the Lloyds Bank site in York and dated to the 9th to 11th c. comes an alder wood shoe last (find no. 494), further demonstrating that the Lloyds Bank site was a leatherworking centre in York during this period.[211] The find confirms that shoe manufacturing was well advanced as a craft during the Anglo-Saxon period.

---

[209] Ottaway, 1992
[210] Hirst & clark, 2009
[211] MacGregor, 1982

4 Tool Finds by Occupation

Smaller Hand Tools – Gouges, Pegs, Awls

York during the Anglian and Anglo-Scandinavian periods has proved a rich source of leatherworkers tools with finds of gouges used in leatherworking (Fishergate 5524)[212] derived from cow bones, along with antler tines from Lloyds Bank (finds 611 to 618)[213] presumed to be tanners' pegs[214] and used in a similar fashion to the later medieval iron tenterhooks.

It seems prudent here to investigate the awls of York for they represent a microcosm of awl finds from around Britain at this time. Awls are probably the most widespread tool find, spread among inhumations and settlements alike, a ubiquitous multi-purpose tool with applications in most industries. In a leatherworking context, diamond- and square-section types seem the most prevalent with five diamond-section awls from Fishergate alone.

Fishergate Find No.	Date Range
4948	Late 8th Century
4949	Early 9th Century
4950-52	10th Century

Further finds from the Lloyds Bank site all have a 9th - 11th c. context: finds no. 422 to 425 being of square section and find no. 426 of the much rarer round section, with an average length of 6 to 9 cm (including tang). Reconstructive experiments have shown that the diamond-section awl is a very effective slitting tool for piercing leather, closely followed by the square or rectangular awl. The round-section awl is the least effective but gives a neat, round hole which is not likely to rip.

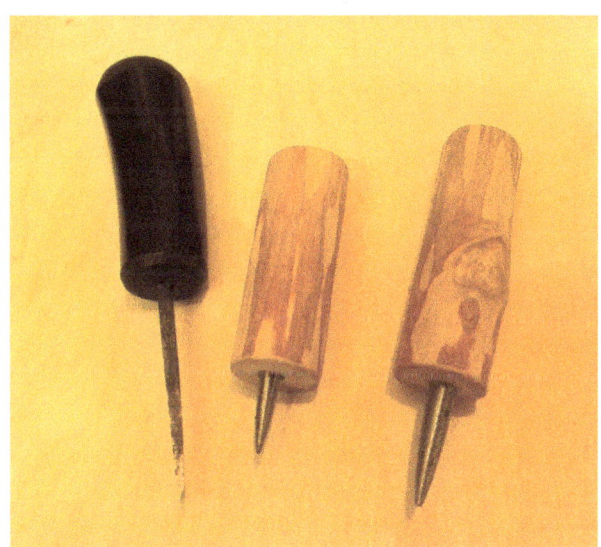

Figure 45
Reproductions of small awls, left: Coppergate (York); middle and right: Tattershal Thorpe

---

[212] Rogers, 1993 p1264
[213] MacGregor, 1982
[214] Postulated by Radley, 1971

4 Tool Finds by Occupation

The awl finds from Coppergate are extensive with no less than fourteen objects described as "tanged punches" (finds 2229-2243 excluding 2236) which may be viewed as a somewhat vague description but a superficial archaeological classification.[215] All these 'punches' can be viewed as awls of some sort with a variety of end uses and cross sections - both round and square. Chief amongst their uses is likely to be leatherworking. The fifteenth tanged punch (find 2244) is of a most unusual design, being flat faced and here again a leatherworking function cannot be ruled out for this tool. Of the eleven awls of diamond cross-section, four (nos. 2718, 2722, 2726 and 2734) have a flattened central section with a taper to each end implying that the tool possibly fitted into some type of socketed handle or holder and could be pulled out and reset reversed, thus extending the life of the awl. If one arm broke, it is probable that the tool would have been set permanently in a wooden handle. All the evidence available points to the awl handle being without a retaining ferrule: indeed, only one awl from Coppergate (no. 2731) was recovered with a ferrule. An unferruled handle can split easily, forcing the awl tang into the hand and potentially causing a debilitating injury - but if the handle were longer than the awl and its tang, the risk of injury is greatly reduced. Of the rectangular or round cross-sectioned awls recovered from Coppergate, the longest (including tang) was find no. 2711 at 68 mm, the shortest being find no .2706 at 32 mm.

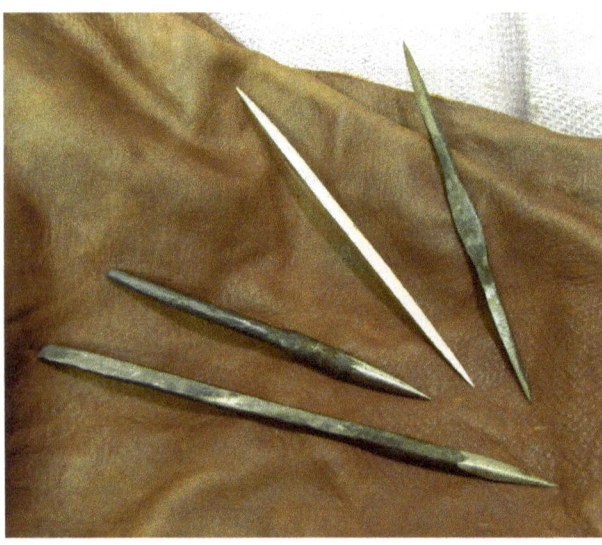

Figure 46
Reproduction leatherworking awls, without handles

Bone- and Antler-Working Tools

The nature of a craft-specific tool is sometimes difficult to define. Most tools have a potential multi-craft function and a leatherworking workshop may carry many of the tools of a bone- or antler-worker. The context of finds is important here, since the working debris from an excavated site and the tools found with it, are often the only indicator of what the tool was actually used for.

---

[215] Ottaway 1992

Bone and antler are of high integral strength, requiring sharp and strong tools to work them. Much of the evidence of tool use comes from the bones themselves: the marks and defects caused by working the material indicate the nature of the tool used and from this evidence we can discern that saws were utilised, as were the ubiquitous awl and the rasp. From decorated finds we can see the use of the ring-and-dot auger for the production of the widespread ring-and-dot pattern adorning many extant bone and antler items and also, in a variant form, used to manufacture bone and antler beads. Although there are no extant ring-and-dot augers or boring augers, their existence is inferred from their tool signatures.

Saws

It seems that the Anglo-Saxons had little interest in using the saw for primary or secondary woodwork, the axe serving them well in this respect, but bone is much harder and the saw is ideally suited to working this difficult material. Saws from the Anglo-Saxon period are a rare item and, in this context, we have four examples which are likely to have had a bone- or antler-working function. From the 8th and 9th c.(Middle Saxon period) comes a saw from the National Portrait Gallery site (London) with five teeth per inch.[216] We do not know if the saw had a set (the alternating left/right angling of the teeth to make the saw cut wider than the thickness of the saw blade). The presence of a set is not crucial to the use of a saw as experiments have shown an unset saw works well at cutting but the blade does require a slight side-to-side motion to make the slot wider than the blade body to prevent binding in the slot. The London blade is unfortunately incomplete, so we cannot say if the blade had a handle or was used like a modern bow- or frame-saw.

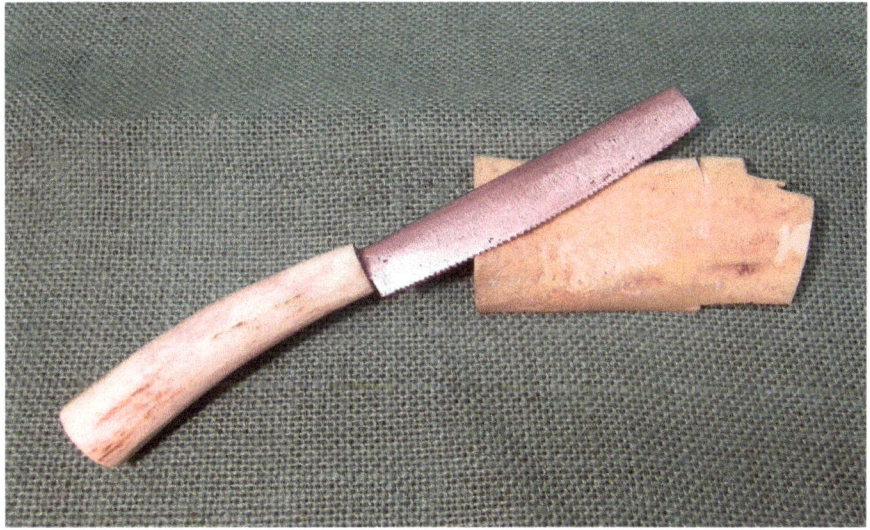

Figure 47 Reproduction of the Coppergate saw, find 283

---

[216] Leary,2004

From the 9th-10th c, deposits at Coppergate (York) comes a bow-saw handle made of antler (find no. 7704),[217] unfortunately minus its blade, consisting of a bowed antler shaft forming the handle with a peg inserted into a hole halfway along the spine with the blade fitting between the peg and the end. A bone- and antler-working function is likely for this saw as the handle is decorated with graffiti in the form of cuts and ring-and-dot work. Also from Coppergate comes find 2983,[218] a converted knife with a squared-off tip (experiments show this allows for an easy stab-free grip between thumb and forefinger) with teeth intervals at 13-14 per 10 mm, again with a likely bone- and antler-working context.

From Mitchell's Hill,[219] Icklingham (Suffolk) comes a saw with an iron case (now in the Ashmolean Museum) of eight teeth per inch which appears to be complete at 14.7 cm long. Of interest here is that the saw has no obvious means of being held - neither by a handle nor in a frame. It is possible (as reconstructions have shown) that the saw can be held between thumb and forefinger of both hands and used in this manner for sawing. It may be a residual or possibly re-used Roman example.

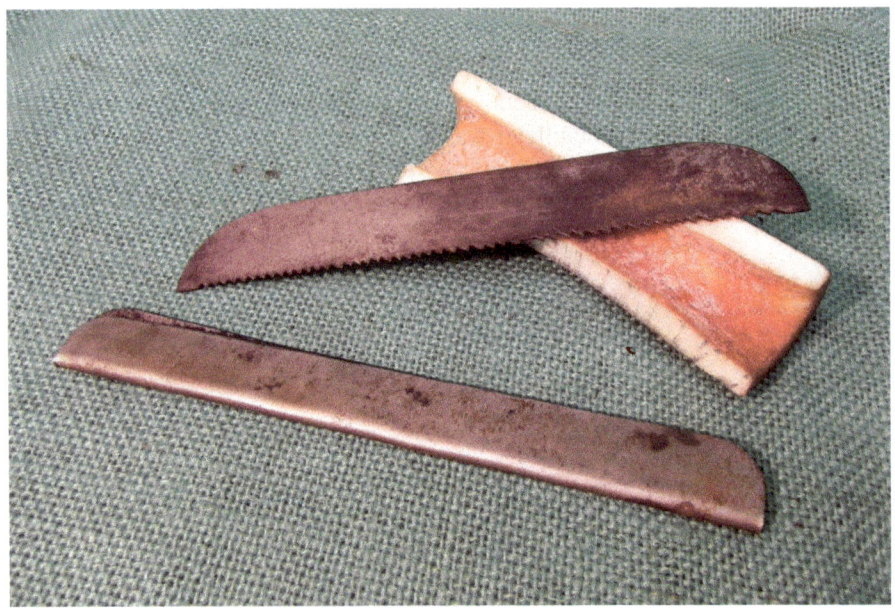

Figure 48 Reproduction of the Icklingham saw

---

[217] MacGregor, Mainman & Rogers, 1999
[218] Ottaway, 1992
[219] West, 1998

Rasps

An indispensable tool of the bone- and antler-worker is the rasp, a coarse-toothed version of the finer metalworkers' file. Such finds from Britain are however scarce, currently only three are known, all from the occupation site at Flixborough (Lincolnshire) two of which are unstratified (finds 2427 and 2428).[220] The datable find (no. 2429) is dated to the 8th-late 9th c. and is small at only 8 mm wide and 66 mm long, including tang. This rasp has two interesting points: firstly, it is cross-cut (which is to say it has two sets of cut teeth set at an angle to each other) and secondly it has a convex curve to the tooth face which would seem odd. However experimental archaeology has shown that a curved rasp is more effective at material removal than its straight counterpart due to each tooth being more exposed on the curved example. Bone- and antler-working rasps, by their very nature, require a coarse cut to the teeth to stop the residual material from clogging them. The tooth distance on the Flixborough examples varies between 4 and 8 teeth per cm.

Figure 49
Reproduction of the Flixborough rasp, find 2429

Awls

The use of awls is attested in bone- and antler-working for the decorative shaping of the material, and here the knife could have been utilised for the same purpose.

From the Middle Saxon deposits at the Royal Opera House (London) comes a square-section awl some 7.5 cm long found with antler waste, so its context would support its use in bone- and-antler working.[221] It is dated to 730-770 AD. It is interesting to note that this particular find (M53) is made from copper alloy. Depending upon their composition, copper alloys can be as hard as steel, and a reconstructed awl in high tensile brass (copper/zinc alloy) shows that its marking abilities in some respects exceed that of steel when working bone. As has already been stated, awls can and do have a multitude of applications and it is only the context of an awl find (the residual waste) that can determine its use.

---

[220] Evans & Loveluck, 2009
[221] Malcolm, Bowsher & Cowie, 2003

4 Tool Finds by Occupation

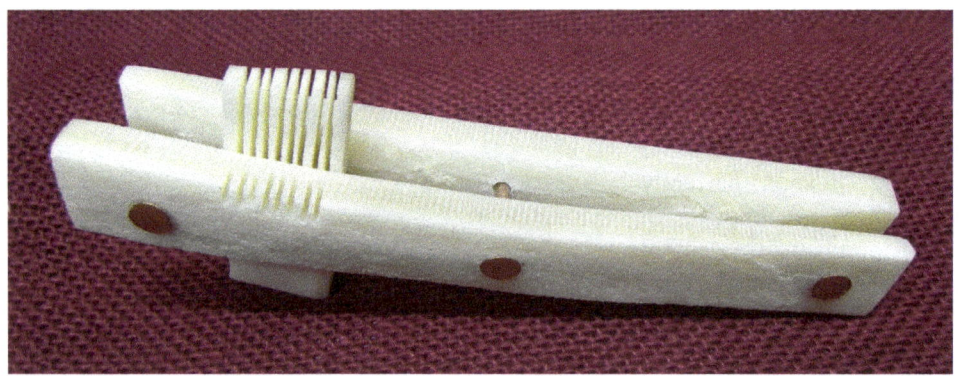

Figure 50 Reproduction riveted mount with sawn bone plate in situ showing saw grooving on the mount

Rivetted Mounts

Not all tools are easy to define as to function, and the so called 'rivetted mounts' are a case in point.[222] Excavated in Coppergate (York) was a series of mounts each consisting of two bone or antler parallel plates connected by rivets - usually three, but in some cases two with a gap between them - dating from the 8th-9th c. (find 6917) up to the 15th c. (find 6957). Forty-one finds in total spread throughout the Anglo-Scandinavian period into the medieval period, they are crudely constructed with regular saw marks usually on one edge. The presumption has been that they are some sort of gripping tool for holding plates of horn, antler or bone perhaps for sawing before refitting into a similar but better quality set of scale plates. This is entirely feasible as pre-cutting the teeth avoids marking the finished comb scale plates. Some of the riveted mounts have decoration, but here it is entirely possible that they had been used as practice plates for working out design. The longevity of the item would suggest a tool rather than a fashion accessory. Another similar find comes from Bishopstone (Sussex) (find 30) contemporary with the early Coppergate finds and decorated with cross hatching.[223] The latter detail could be for grip whilst cutting the teeth. The piece also has the regular saw nicks seen on the Coppergate finds, so a tool function seems likely here as well.

---

[222] MacGregor et al, 1999
[223] Thomas, 2010

Clamps

Availability of suitable materials often dictates tool design and, in an industry utilising bone and antler, it is likely that as many tools as possible would exploit the offcuts of the comb-making process. This is also shown by the use of bone and antler vice clamps from Coppergate (York) with three well preserved examples.

Find No.		
7745	82.1mm long	930-975AD
7746	91mm long	930-975AD
7747	94.8mm long	975AD - 11th c.

Figure 51 Reproduction Coppergate-style bone clamp with a wooden wedge

The construction of the vice clamp is simple: two plates are loosely riveted together in the middle, the workpiece is secured between the clamps at one end and a wedge of bone, antler or wood is forced in the other with the loose rivet acting as the fulcrum. Reconstructions show it to be an effective holding tool for working on small items. This type of clamp is documented in Scandinavia with finds from Hedeby,[224] Iceland and elsewhere.[225] There is a similar clamp from a "smith's" grave at Ytre Elgsnes[226] but here the grave contents could also have functioned as a comb-makers tool-set.[227]

---

[224] Ulbricht, 1978
[225] MacGregor, 1985
[226] Simonsen, 1953
[227] Tempel, 1969

4 Tool Finds by Occupation

It is sometimes difficult to know what constitutes a 'tool' and what constitutes 'scrap'. In reconstructing tools and techniques of the Anglo-Saxon period I have used off-cuts of bone and antler as plattens, wedges and supports for a variety of items. It is likely that some of the fragments recovered from the Anglo-Scandinavian deposits in York (principally Coppergate) would have had a secondary tool function, although what that function may have been is beyond present knowledge. Thus it is prudent to adopt a policy of exclusion, since speculative use of tools serves little purpose except to challenge our ingenuity in finding uses for apparently useless items!

Textile-Workers' Tools

By 'textile workers' we mean 'women'! 'Textile production was largely – perhaps exclusively - the preserve of females of various ages. Women and weaving have a deep-rooted, ancient and complex relationship related in some respects to social position. Whereas it can be argued that a man's relationship with the tools he used was largely impersonal, a woman's relationship was anything but: the tools of her trade were highly individual items, to such an extent that in many female graves at least one or more weaving-related item was included, in comparison to male graves where tools are very rare.

In view of the complexity of the relationship and the breadth of the subject we will adopt a sequential view of the processing of raw material to finished garment. There were two main fabric sources: animal-derived and plant-derived materials. 'Animal-derived' effectively means sheep's wool, while the plant material is largely confined to flax and hemp. There is some evidence for the use of the stinging nettle but it was apparently little used in textile manufacture.[228] Both flax and hemp utilise the same equipment and in the main have the same production methods.

Flax fibres run the length of the plant, all of which can be harvested for processing. The flax stems are cut and dried then pulled through a ripple to remove the seed pods; a ripple is a large wooden comb with stout teeth. This process reduces the flax to a single stem ready for retting which involves the microbial rotting of the entire plant in a still-water environment, normally over several weeks.[229] The plant stems are removed from the water and dried to render the bark brittle for pounding, whereby the stems are broken with a flax pounder (a round mallet).

Removal of the bark is handled using a scutching knife. The pounded fibres are laid a vertical board and the scutching knife brought down against the fibres to the bottom of the board. This removes the bark fragments (or 'shives' as they are called) leaving the sub-surface fibres intact. The resulting semi-processed bundle is called "tow". The next process turns the mass of tow into individual fibres by drawing through a heckle - a series of long, sharp iron teeth. On archaeological sites it can be hard to distinguish between wool comb teeth and heckle teeth, although heckle teeth are generally larger than wool comb teeth. Wool combs are used by hand while

---

[228] Walton Rogers, 2007 p15.
[229] Walton Rogers, 2007

heckles are bench-mounted.[230] Another feature to assist with identification is that wool combs are used within settlement areas whereas heckling is more often undertaken on the outskirts of a settlement due to its dusty nature. Hence location is an aid to determining the function of finds. The processing of hemp utilises exactly the same process as flax manufacture, with the same equipment being employed.

The production of wool is a series of simple tasks: the sheep is shorn and the fibres separated into the fine and coarse wool; the shorn wool can be spun "in the grease" straight from the animal but it is more usual to clean the wool in detergents and re-oil it before spinning to give a good quality thread.

Primary Wool Processing Tools

Shears

To produce wool ready for spinning it needs first to be cut from the animal; for which shears are used. Archaeologically, it is difficult to separate sheep shears from household shears and it is likely that they were the same tools. It would seem probable that the larger shears were used for this process as small, short shears would increase the shearing time and distress to both animal and shearer.

Shears can be manufactured left- or right-handed (see p.19ff) and, as anyone who has tried shears can attest, it makes little difference to the functionality of the tool as it can be used in either hand. This is due to the nature of the tool: scissors are made left- or right-handed to match the hand of the user because the blade and hand are separated by the fulcrum (the pivot point of the scissors). As scissors are closed, the blades are also forced together but if used in the wrong hand the blades are forced apart as they close. With shears this does not occur as the fulcrum is at the rear which causes the blades to be forced together whichever hand is used. Thus to some degree the handedness of shears should be random, but this is not the case. The archaeological evidence points to shears having been manufactured predominantly left-handed, and there are a number of possible reasons for this:

1. Archaeology. The finds are disproportionately left-handed. This might be attributed to the shears being unsprung prior to burial to protect the blades from biting into each other. Nevertheless, the set of the blades shown in the archaeological drawings indicates that they are designed for left-handed use. Unless there is evidence to the contrary, we must assume that the archaeological record reflects items used in life – with all the usual caveats about grave-goods offering a formal and selective view of the deceased.

2. Genetics. As discussed above (p.19), research shows that there appears to be a genetic factor (the LRRTM1 gene) which determines handedness.[231]

3. Acquired behaviour. This may be called 'nurture over nature'. As mentioned previously, an ambidextrous individual is likely to be more of an asset to a community than a unidexter.

---

[230] Walton Rogers, 2007
[231] Franks et al, Molecular Psychiatry, (2007) 12:1129-1139

4. Manufacturing bias. It might be chance that more left-handed shears were made than right-handed shears, due to the preferences of the smiths.

5. Method of use. It is possible that the Anglo-Saxons used their shears in a way that modern man does not. For instance, with vertical weaving looms a right-handed user would naturally cut fabric from right to left because it is easier to determine the path of the cut.

Whatever the actual reason(s) the evidence of the finds shows that over twice as many shears were apparently constructed left-handed as right handed (where a determination of handedness can be made).[232]

Tools change over time, sometimes quickly with the introduction of an innovation but more usually slowly due to changing materials being used. Dating a tool by its construction is difficult, not least because each one is an individually crafted item that loosely corresponds to a design norm. In this respect, shears are no different from any other tool. Shears exhibit two constructional types: those with a U-shaped spring bend (the fulcrum) and those with the so called omega bend (Ω). The U-shaped type is usually allocated an early to middle Anglo-Saxon date[233] and the omega type to a later Saxon date.[234] However this should be regarded as a trend rather than a fixed seriation.

The evidence from the Anglo-Saxon cemetery and settlement at Bloodmoor Hill, Carlton Coleville (Norfolk)[235] shows the omega loop in use and dated to the 7th century (finds 355 and fragments of 351/2). Indeed, all the finds of shears from Bloodmoor Hill show a variety of forms from the U to the omega. This synchronous use of both types suggests that no chronological transition between the two took place.

Shears are a functional item with the design dictated by the need for them to work efficiently rather than a style or fashion to be followed. The extant finds show the shear loops and the cutting angles of the blades vary markedly, they also correspond well with my reconstructed examples as they are difficult to set while still looking attractive. The principal requirement is not appearance but performance.

The general size of shears is remarkably consistent throughout the Anglo-Saxon period, ranging in the majority of cases from around 150 mm to 200 mm in length with a cutting blade of 40 - 50% of the overall length. The major exceptions to this are to be found in cremation urns of the Migration Period, for example the finds from Spong Hill[236] where the shears are likely to have been constructed as purpose-made funerary items manufactured to fit into the urn. The size of many of the Spong Hill shears is around 100 mm (i.e. about half the size of standard shears) and with

---

[232] Riley, 2011
[233] Ottaway, 1992
[234] Ottaway, 1992, p548. Walton-Rogers, 1997, p 1781.
[235] Lucy, Tipper & Dickens, 2009
[236] Hills, 1997; report no 6, Hills & Penn, 1981: report no 11

4 Tool Finds by Occupation

thick arms, even allowing for the effects of oxidation on the iron, which calls into question their functionality.

Even in the funerary context, the shears have been constructed predominantly for left-handed use. In view of the quantity found in these early cemetery sites, it is apparent that the inclusion of shears formed an important part of the funerary rite and is likely to be a status indicator, not necessarily related to wealth but perhaps to the social function and importance of the owner in the provision of cloth for the community.

Iron Shears Find spot	Find Ref.	Date (Century)	Total length mm	Blade length mm	Blade % of total length
Bloodmoor Hill cemetery	G11	6-8th	180	90	50
Bloodmoor Hill cemetery	G12	6-8th	148	70	48
Bloodmoor Hill occupation	353	6-8th	152	70	46
Bloodmoor Hill occupation	354	6-8th	200	80	40
Bloodmoor Hill occupation	355	6-8th	192	90	47
Harford Farm	G11	Late 7th	200	80	40
Harford Farm	G18	Late 7th	170	70	41
Harford Farm	G20	Late 7th	160	70	44
Harford Farm	G33	Late 7th	180	66	37
Spong Hill	1824	Early 7th	85	50	58
Spong Hill	1950	Early 7th	90	35	38
Spong Hill	2036	Early 7th	75	35	46
Spong Hill	2078	Early 7th	85	30	35
Spong Hill	1696	Early 7th	155	65	42
Spong Hill	1961	Early 7th	170?	60	35
Spong Hill	2169	Early 7th	180	90	50
Flixborough Occupation	2859	8-9th	188	60	32
Flixborough Occupation	2861	10-11th	143	46	32
Flixborough Occupation	2871	9th	160	56	35
Flixborough Occupation	2877	9th	191	70	36
Flixborough Occupation	2879	10-11th	185	74	40
Finglesham cemetery	G57	6-8th	150	60	40
Finglesham cemetery	G138	6-8th	160	50	31
Finglesham cemetery	G150	6-8th	160	70	44
Finglesham cemetery	G8	6-8th	180	80	44

4 Tool Finds by Occupation

The finds listed in the table above are a sample from a number of sites, as indicated. It is interesting to note that it appears, on the basis of the Flixborough finds, that there is a change around the 9th c. to a shorter blade. This may be merely coincidental in view of the small sample. The table entries for Spong Hill list only the full-size functional shears. It should be borne in mind that dozens of shears were recovered from this extensive inhumation and cremation cemetery, but many of the shears were probably intended as symbolic grave-goods.

As with the general evidence regarding the handedness of shears, from the four finds listed for Finglesham three examples are for left-handed use; the grave 8 find was unsprung and of indeterminate handedness.

Wool Cards

After the wool has been removed from the sheep and cleaned, it needs carding. Modern cards are a series of short fine wires set in a fabric matrix in their hundreds, designed to tease out the fibres of the wool in a parallel direction ready for spinning. Anglo-Saxon females were not obliged to use such flimsy tools in their daily life as we satisfy ourselves with, and the Anglo-Saxon wool card was a sturdy tool built to last.

Outlined below is selection of the card finds from Anglo-Saxon England. The wool card was generally a wooden block with a handle into which are set two parallel rows of teeth, usually 10 to 20 in number. The teeth are normally around 80 to 100 mm long spacing of about 5 to 10 mm and about 10 mm between the rows, which are offset so that no tooth is directly behind another. The wooden head is usually encased in iron casing to both flat faces and the edges, giving a robust tool that should last a lifetime. A feature of these cards is that they are very heavy, due to the amount of metalwork used.

Experimental archaeologists and re-enactors often find difficulty in using a reconstructed pair of cards, as modern wrists not often used to such heavy work, giving rise to the perception that Anglo-Saxon women were heavily muscled around the forearm and wrist area. According to Walton-Rogers[237] *"they are difficult for re-enactors to reconstruct"*, which is borne out by my own recreations. Although a technically simple tool, they are labour-intensive to manufacture, especially with the re-enforcing iron sheath. Walton-Rogers adds that they are generally found in well-furnished graves and that they therefore carried some prestige value. Indeed, given the difficulty of manufacturing, only the wealthy could afford to be buried with a pair, as a second set must have remained in use.

Finds of carding combs in settlement areas (usually as comb tooth fragments inside buildings) increase from the 7th c. onwards, possibly indicating that textile production became more communal and centralised.

---

[237] Walton-Rogers, 1997, 1720-1

Wool Card Finds

Site	Reference	Date	Remarks
Butlers Field cemetery	Grave 14	Late 5th- Late 7th C	2 rows of 11 teeth, 100 mm long in an iron case, female, 14-16yrs.
Bloodmoor Hill cemetery	Grave 11	6th to 8th C	2 rows of 9 teeth, 100 mm long, female sub adult/adult.
Flixborough occupation	Find 2504	Unstratified 7-11th C	Teeth 90 mm long and other fragments.
Bishopstone occupation	Find 87	8- late 11th C	2 rows of teeth 14 front, 12 back, 90 mm long iron case.
Coppergate occupation	Find 2273	9th C	2 rows of 16? Teeth 105 mm long iron case.

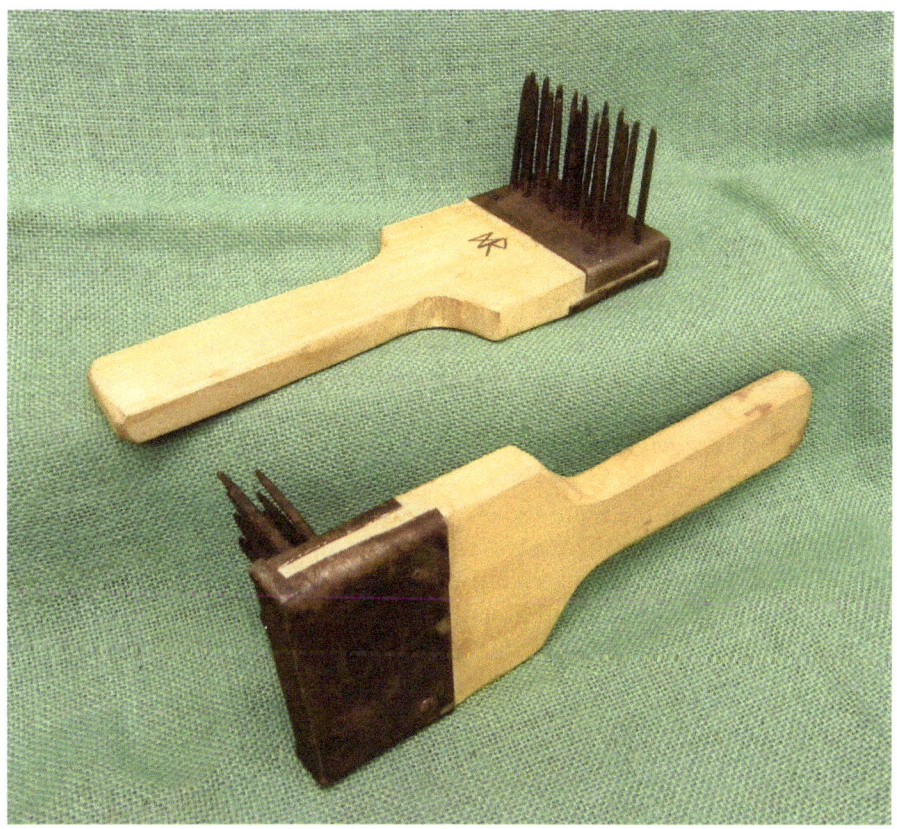

Figure 52 Reproduction wool cards

Other wool comb finds come from the Milk Street site in London, dated to the 9th-11th century (unpublished, Museum of London), a pair from Wicken Bonhunt (Essex)[238] and from a Viking burial in Harrold, Bedfordshire[239] but it is possible in the latter case that it may be the remains of a flax heckle.

The possibility of wooden wool combs being employed during the Anglo-Saxon period in England should not be overlooked although their use is speculative since wood does not survive well. There is a continental find from the 11th century deposits at Novgorod (Russia) where it appears a large comb with coarse teeth held the wool and a finer, smaller comb was employed to draw out the fibres from the wool.[240] If such a device had been in use in Britain at this time, little evidence if any would have survived.

Interestingly there is a wall painting from Pompeii of a woman using a wool comb set in a wooden block used in a similar fashion to those found in Viking and early medieval Novgorod; with such a long continuous and wide spread use, their use in Anglo-Saxon Britain is therefore possible.

Primary Plant Fibre Processing Tools

As has been previously discussed, the main plant fibres used for cloth during the Anglo-Saxon period were flax and hemp and their processing routes were largely the same. The method involves three main processes: rippling, pounding and scutching - all requiring a considerable degree of effort to produce strands ready for spinning.

Ripplers

Once the flax has been cut, it requires the seed pods to be removed and saved for next year's crop. This task was handled using a rippler, which is essentially a large-toothed wooden comb with the distance between the tines large enough to accept the stalk but not the seed head. There are no known Anglo-Saxon finds from Britain of this type of tool, the earlies one we have is find no. 6641 from the 13th century levels at Coppergate, York, made from pinewood with five tines with a total width of around 8cm.[241] The rippler is designed to sit in a larger wooden block in the field so that rippling can take place at the point of harvesting prior to retting. The Coppergate rippler is likely to be a Norwegian import due to its pine construction, and it has the same style and construction as some finds from Bergen (Norway) dated to 1170-1332 AD.[242] Given that there are 1st century AD finds from Roman *Vindonissa* (Switzerland) of similar wooden construction, it seems likely that the Anglo-Saxons had a similar device.[243] This wooden tool seems to have had a long production run.

---

[238] Edwards, 1975.
[239] Eagles & Evison 1970.
[240] Brisbane & Hather (editors), 2007 p 140
[241] Morris, 2000
[242] Øye, 1988
[243] Øye, 1988

4 Tool Finds by Occupation

Pounders

As the name suggests, this type of tool was used for pounding the flax to remove the outer hard layer of woody material and to release the fibre bundles within. The flax was first pre-treated by retting which involves laying bundles of the rippled flax in still water for up to six weeks to partially rot the outer bark of the plant. Once the retting process is finished the partially rotten (and foul smelling) flax is removed and dried, usually over some sort of kiln to embrittle the bark ready for pounding. It is likely that the rippling and retting stages of flax production would have been a male-oriented occupation, with the pounding stage moving to the female side for continued processing.

Flax pounders are round wooden mallets used to break the bark from the plant stems, of which a couple of Anglo-Saxon examples are known. The Anglo-Scandinavian levels at Coppergate[244] (York) yielded two such pounders (no. 6642 made from willow. dated to 975-mid 11th c. and no. 6643 made from alder, dated to the mid to late 11th c.). There are also finds from Viking Dublin and 12th c. Perth (Scotland) and an oak example some 340 mm long (including the 200 mm head) from a retting pit or well at Westbury (Buckinghamshire) dated to the 7th -8th c.[245] Scandinavian finds from this period include those from the 9th c. Oseberg (Norway) ship burial, the 11th c. levels at Lund (Sweden), and Viking levels at Hedeby and Novgorod.

Scutching Knives

The scutching knife is a flat-bladed paddle used to remove the bark fragments from the flax. The flax bundles are held in the hand against a vertical board set into the ground and the scutching knife is brought down against the flax. There are at least three examples from Anglo-Saxon England: Coppergate[246] (York) find no. 6644, dated to 975-mid 11th c., made of oak with a paddle construction (two blades); a find from Kings Lynn (Norfolk)[247] and another from Macclesfield (Cheshire)[248]. Continental finds come from Hedeby (Denmark) and Viking period Novgorod (Russia).[249] It is interesting to note that many of the Novgorod finds are single-bladed like a weaving sword or batten but with a serrated edge: these may represent hemp scutchers the bark of which is more difficult to remove by scutching, the serrations aiding in the bark removal, although this is speculative.

---

[244] Morris, 2000.
[245] Ivens et al, 1995.
[246] Morris, 2000.
[247] Clarke & Carter, 1997
[248] Morris 1984a.
[249] Kolchin,1989. Refer also to Brisbane & hather (Ed), 2007

4 Tool Finds by Occupation

Figure 53 Reproduction scutching, pounding and rippling tools

Heckles

Once scutched, the fibres require heckling through a series of pins to shred the fibres into thinner and finer strands. Each set of heckles through which the fibres pass is finer than the previous set, until they are of the required size. Alternatively the heckle may be made a set of pins, as many deep as they are wide, and the flax is drawn through the pins until the fibres are down to size.

Distinguishing heckle pins from wool comb pins is difficult, although there is a presumption that heckle pins are larger. Heckles are not hand-held but set into a plank or bench for hand-drawing. No complete heckle from Anglo-Saxon England has been found, so the exact construction is speculative but presumed heckle pins have been found at Flixborough (Lincolnshire), West Heslerton (Yorkshire) and Harrold (Bedfordshire).[250] Opinion is divided in the latter instance, with Geake proposing that the finds are heckle pins and not wool comb pins.

Fabric Processing Tools

Once in their processed, state the wool, flax or hemp requires conversion into cloth. The first stage in this process is spinning. These materials can be spun "dry" but for ease of manufacture they can all be pre-oiled. In the case of wool, it can be spun "in the grease" which is to say, direct from the sheep. Normally however the wool is first cleaned, carded and re-oiled.

---

[250] Geake, 1997 p 61-2

There is a possible oiling ladle recovered from Wicken Bonhunt (Essex) around 20 mm deep, 8 cm wide and 30cm long with a tanged handle;[251] it was found with a pair of carding combs from the same site. Such a context would imply a textile-making use. The fibres, whether oiled or unoiled, are now ready for spinning and this is where the status of the worker is made evident.

Figure 54 Reproduction of the Wicken Bonhunt oiling ladle

Spinning Tools

Spinning, like most textile production, was the domain of females both old and young. From grave finds it seems the allotted task in the process could change with the importance of the individual female within the family unit. It seems likely that girls would learn to spin from a very early age, a skill that would occupy much of their time throughout their lives.

The only known spinning tool from the Anglo-Saxon period in England is the drop-spindle, a round weight or flywheel set towards the lower end of a round-section wooden shaft perhaps 200 to 300 mm in length. The material used for the weight or 'whorl' could include pottery, glass, bone, antler, stone and wood (although no wooden spindle whorls are known to survive).

Spindle whorls are one of the few tool items copiously represented in female burials, from which it is assumed that they were personal items. Being often relatively cheap and easy to make, even the poorest family could furnish the dead with such a parting gift. It is not certain that the whorls were on their shafts at the point of burial, as the woodwork does not survive.

Spindle whorls can be classified as A, B or C series whorls on the basis of cross-sectional shape. This method of classification was first adopted for the excavation at Coppergate (York) and since then has been extended to capture sub groups.[252] Dating tools by form alone is always difficult since many are unique items and numerous types were in use simultaneously. The types reproduced here were in common use throughout the Anglo-Saxon period and have been reduced to the most basic shapes.

---

[251] Ottaway, n.d.
[252] Walton-Rogers, 2007, p 24-25

4 Tool Finds by Occupation

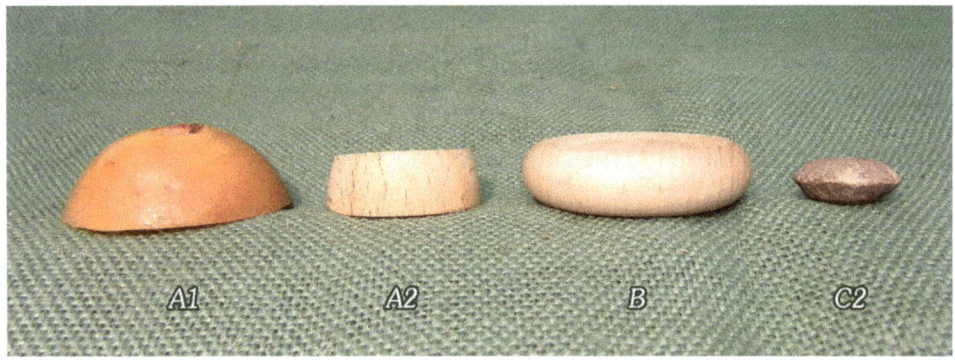

Figure 55 Reproduction spindle whorl classification by profile

Type **Description**
- A1   Hemispherical with one flat face
- A2   Unequal flat face; one face is a larger diameter than the other, with conical sides
- B   Equal flat faces, barrel or disc shaped
- C2   Ovoid or rhombic in cross section to varying degrees

The material used to make spindle whorls varies, as mentioned previously. There is an assumption that turned wooden whorls were made, although none are known to survive. Bone was used in the form of cattle femur heads - once cut they readily conform to a type A whorl. Antler was used in the form of the burr head, and clay (fired as pottery) could be produced to any shape. There are finds of stone and shale, turned on the bow lathe to types A2, B and C2, and of cast lead, smaller than the non-metal finds and usually of a type C2 profile. Some of the bone examples are decorated with incised lines and the ubiquitous ring-and-dot motif. The turned examples often bear concentric grooves and the cast lead examples some linear decoration. There does seem to be some preference or social constraint within cemetery finds as to the material employed in construction, whereby one type predominates over all others within the cemetery. This may be due to local availability of materials or to cultural taste.

Further analysis of cemetery finds set against the age of the owner at the time of burial, reveals an interesting age-related use of the spindle whorl, with a peak in the incidence of such burial in the 20 to 30 years age range. This may be due to the owner being in her prime and head female of the household and thus also the head of the community's spinners. This may imply that spinning was her main priority in textile production, with wool and fibre preparation undertaken by the young and old in a subordinate function. The possession of the spindle whorl could therefore be viewed as a status-marker within the community.

Spindle shafts of wood do not survive archaeologically, but there is evidence that shafts could also be made of iron. There is a number of possible finds including a tapered rod some 200 mm long from Swallowcliffe Down (Wiltshire)[253] found in a burial casket but without a spindle whorl; as the shaft was iron, the whorl may have been of wooden construction and therefore would not survive. Further examples include a casket from grave 299 at Kingston Down (Kent)[254] containing two iron spindles (along with spindle whorls) and another iron spindle from Wingham (Kent).[255] As an interesting Continental parallel, there are surviving wooden spindle shafts from medieval Novgorod (Russia)[256] dating from the 12th to 14th c. Since the drop-spindle has not changed materially over time, it is likely that these survivors are like those used in England during the Anglo-Saxon period. They vary in length from 20 to 30 cm and generally taper to both ends from the thickest point around one-third of the way up the shaft. There is one example that was parallel-sided.

Figure 56 Reproduction spindle whorls of bone, lead and pottery

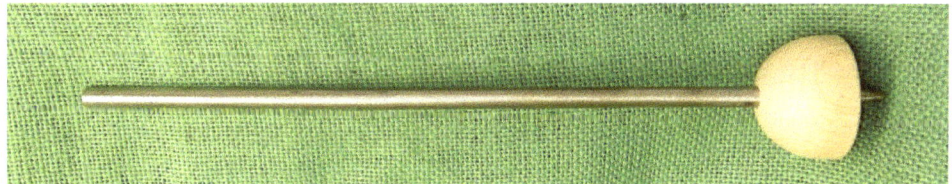

Figure 57 Reproduction of the Swallowcliffe Down iron spindle shaft and whorl

---

[253] Speake, 1989
[254] Faussett, 1856
[255] Akerman, 1855
[256] Brisbane & Hather (eds), 2007

4 Tool Finds by Occupation

Weaving Tools

Having produced spun thread, the next stage in production involves weaving the threads on a loom. During the Anglo-Saxon period the main weaving loom was the vertical warp weaving frame on which tension was maintained on the threads by means of a series of loom weights. These were blocks made of ceramic (either fired or unfired) to which the vertical threads (warp) were tied, and are the main surviving evidence for the use of this type of loom. The characteristically doughnut-shaped loom weight finds are often found in rows where the weaving shed has been destroyed by fire, so the length and overall size of these looms can be determined from the disposition of the weights. The warp-weighted loom is associated with two types of tool: the pin-beater (or 'thread-picker') and the weaving batten (also called a 'slay' or 'sword'). Both types of tools disappear from the archaeological record by the late Anglo-Saxon period, along with evidence of loom weights, probably indicating a gradual shift to the horizontal weaving loom.[257]

The pin-beater or thread-picker is a cigar-shaped object, thick in the middle and tapering points which are highly polished (due to wear in use) with the central portion quite rough for ease of handling. They are designed to pick out the thread during weaving, to ensure that the cloth is of a consistent quality and free of defects. These pin-beaters are made from bone or antler, although it is possible that wooden versions existed but do not survive archaeologically. Experimental reconstructions of wooden pin-beaters in elder have shown that they could take a good degree of polish by burnishing, making an acceptable tool for textile use, but there is no evidence that wooden pin-beaters were used.

Figure 58 Reproduction smaller pin-beater from Dover Buckland grave 75, possibly intended for use with linen

Pin-beaters were probably personal items for females, as is shown by the inhumation burial evidence which is small but significant. In a burial context these tools are rarely found in isolation but usually in a collection or "kit" of weaving equipment which in some cases can comprise a number of pin-beaters, spindle whorls and shears. It follows that females were considerably more likely to be buried with their craft tools than males, but this may be due to economic factors (textile-working tools being more numerous than smithing tools.)

---

[257] Walton-Rogers, 2007

4 Tool Finds by Occupation

A high proportion of females could have an extensive array of whorls and pin-beaters in their graves, which poses the question 'why are more sets of tools not found?' Here we can assume that burial practice plays a large part, as does the structure of Anglo-Saxon society with only senior weavers and those of high social status being accorded such honour.

Archaeological evidence indicates that pin-beaters fall into two sizes: a shorter group of around 10 cm in length and a longer of around 15cm, with very few finds falling between these groups. Such a distribution would imply two separate tool types and Walton Rogers makes the point that the smaller type may have been used in linen production.[258]

Stray finds of pin-beaters are usually found in isolation which is the natural consequence of casual loss; even so, in settlements the finds are usually made in the vicinity of textile-working buildings.

Pin-Beater finds, early to late Anglo-Saxon period

Find Spot	Date	Remarks
Bloodmoor Hill	Late 7th -8th c.	Fragments of 4 pin-beaters from the Settlement area
Dover Buckland	Late 5th -mid 8th c	Cemetery find grave 75, 9.7cm long
Finglesham	6th -8th c.	Cemetery find grave 8, 14.4cm long
Finglesham	6th -8th c.	Cemetery find grave 180, 9.45cm long Constructed from gunmetal (copper alloy)
Flixborough	8-9th C	Settlement area - two finds
Flixborough	Early/mid 9th c.	Settlement area - one find
Flixborough	Mid-late 9th c.	Settlement area - one find
Flixborough	Early 10th -11th c.	Settlement area - three finds
Flixborough	unstratified	Settlement area - five finds
Royal Opera House London	730-770AD	Building 36, decorated bone pin-beater 18 cm long
Royal Opera House London	730-770AD	Building 27, bone pin-beater Find B88
Royal Opera House London	730-770AD	Open area 26, bone pin-beater Find B184
Royal Opera House London	850-900AD	Abandonment phase bone pin-beater Find B272
Bishopstone	8th –late 11th c.	Settlement area (SF243) find 88, bone pin-beater 11.0 cm long
Butlers Field	Late 5th - late 7th c	Cemetery Grave 54, 12.9 cm long bone pin-beater
Butlers Field	Late 5th - late 7th c.	Cemetery Grave 107 16.0 cm long bone or antler pin-beater

Outlined above is a number of pin-beater finds and it is of interest that the find from the Anglo-Saxon cemetery at Finglesham (6th-8th c.) of a gunmetal pin beater (copper alloy) raises the question of how many other pins from female burials might

---

[258] Evans & Loveluck, 2009

4 Tool Finds by Occupation

have had a textile-related function. It is possible that those found in bags and not in use on the body as dress ornamentation or fasteners may have had a dual function as both a dress accessory and textile tool.

In addition to the pin-beater, the weaving batten was employed to tamp the woven threads into a tight line, giving a tough even-structured cloth. Weaving batten finds are quite rare with only the iron types surviving, usually in higher status graves. These battens usually fall into two categories - the 'sword' and 'spear' types. In some rare cases they are obviously re-used swords and spearheads of which a fine sword example was found in grave 187 in the Anglo-Saxon cemetery at Butlers Field, Lechlade (Gloucestershire) dated from the 5th to late 7th century.[259] The tool was 542 mm long, including the tang.

In addition, it is likely that there were wooden versions which have not survived. As an interesting aside there is a bone knife recovered from grave 24 at Empingham II (Rutland) Anglo-Saxon cemetery which may have been used as a weaving batten.

Of the sword-type battens, six graves[260] in the Isle of Wight, East Anglia, Bedfordshire and Surrey have all yielded finds, as have thirteen graves in Kent.[261] Of the spear-type, there is a 6th century example from grave 17B at Castledyke South (Humberside)[262] with further examples form West Heslerton (Yorkshire) and Searby (Lincolnshire) and one recovered from a 9th century pit at Coppergate (York) along with an 8th c. helmet. Here, however, it seems that the socketed "spear" batten has been specifically designed for the weaving process rather than converted from a weapon.

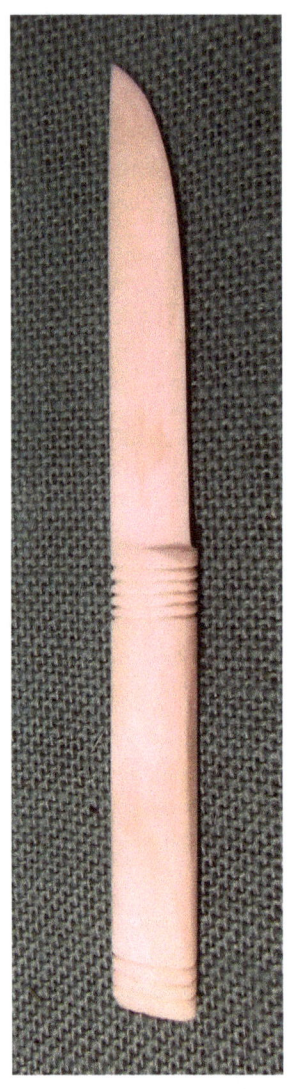

Figure 59 Reproduction bone knife or batten from Empingham II

---

[259] Boyle et al, 1998
[260] Malim and Hines, 1998
[261] Evison, 1987
[262] Drinkall and Foreman, 1998

4 Tool Finds by Occupation

According to Walton-Rogers,[263] weaving battens lengthen with time, in both sword and spear types. From the early to the late Anglo-Saxon period, both types virtually double in length, which may indicate an increase in the width of looms.

Figure 60 Reproduction of the Coppergate weaving batten

From the Anglo-Scandinavian levels at Coppergate (York) comes a probable weaving comb (find no.9179), which was 54 mm long by 44 mm wide, with nine teeth made from either pear, apple or hawthorn wood. The comb would have been used to tamp up the weft instead of the standard batten. If this is the case, it represents a rare find not dissimilar to one found in the Viking Oseberg (Norway) ship burial but more closely resembling weaving combs from the early medieval levels at Novgorod (Russia) of the 12th to 14th c.[264]

Figure 61 Reproduction of the Coppergate weaving comb, find no. 9179

Needles

Once woven, cloth needs to be cut and stitched to make the finished garment. Anglo-Saxon needles were constructed from what was available, which means iron, non-ferrous metals, bone and wood. Although no wooden needles are known to survive from the Anglo-Saxon period, it seems likely that they were in use, being easily and cheaply made. Bone needles were made from the by-products of meat processing, with both pig and cattle bones employed for this purpose. Bone needles are quite crudely constructed and are purely functional items.

Needles were often made from iron, with its high integral strength allowing for small diameters. Non-ferrous (copper alloy) needles are not widespread and, on such small items, non-ferrous metals are not always easy to work especially if they are alloyed (bronze or brass). An exception is a find from the Anglo-Saxon cemetery at Empingham II (Rutland) (grave 85a, find 12) with a copper alloy needle cut from sheet nominally 6 cm long with a punched eye and shank of rectangular cross-section.[265] My reconstruction of this needle shows it had good strength and was very sharp!

---

[263] Walton Rogers, 2007
[264] Brisbane & Hather, 2007 in translation of Kolchin, 1989
[265] Timby, 1996

4 Tool Finds by Occupation

Figure 62 Reproduction of a sheet bronze needle from Empingham II cemetery

It seems wise at this point to look at the manufacturing processes involved in iron needle production which, given the size of product, is quite complicated. The starting point was a length of wire. Modern wire drawing requires high forces to work the material and high purity steel or iron - all three being unavailable to the Anglo-Saxons. The yield strength of iron is around 15 tons per square inch which in simple terms means that to reduce the cross-sectional area of a piece of iron by 1 mm square would require a minimum force of not less than 24 kg. Since the Anglo-Saxons had to rely on the strength of their arms to draw wire, this does raise the question of how they drew the wire from which the needles were manufactured.

Since Anglo-Saxon iron was impure (it contained slag inclusions) it could not have been successfully drawn from a forged ingot (as is modern wire). My experimentation suggests that the likely production method was to forge a piece of iron into a flat, thin sheet around 3 mm thick which then cracks and splits along the slag lines leaving parts of the plate free of slag. These parts are then cut into squares, producing a defect-free sheet. Each sheet is then cut into thin strips, as thick as the metal sheet, producing a needle blank of square section. The blank could then be drawn through a die to round off the edges, with progressive drawing producing a needle blank of round cross-section. Alternatively, the square-section blank could be worked with a hone.

Once the blank has been made, the eye must be inserted - for this, the tip would be annealed and forged flat, re-annealed and the eye worked in. Either of two methods could be employed: the eye could be punched in, leaving a bump on the opposite face which could be ground flat, then the tip would then be punched from the ground side until a hole was forced through forming the eye. Alternatively, the flattened end could be cut with clippers and opened up to form a Y-shaped slot, with both arms being forced over and "welded" closed, thus forming the eye. The evidence suggests that the Anglo-Saxons used both methods but in general the punching method was favoured and gained in popularity as the Anglo-Saxon period progressed.[266] Another possible production route for Y-style eyes is that the entire needle could be made in two D shaped halves and forge-welded together.[267] In view of the small sizes this does seem unlikely, although post-medieval (16th c.) netting needle finds in copper alloy were manufactured in this way by soldering the two halves together.

Needle finds are confined to occupation sites, with the examples cited here being from Coppergate and Fishergate in York and Flixborough in Lincolnshire. From the Anglo-Scandinavian levels at Coppergate (9th - 10th c.) come 150 needles or parts thereof. These Coppergate needles vary from 23 to 73 mm in length and 2 to 3 mm in width measured at the eye, with the smallest needles recorded (find nos. 2464, 2466, 2520 and 2590) being 1 to 1.5mm wide.[268] From the 8th - 9th c. deposits at Fishergate in York come a number of bone needles with a likely textile function (find nos. 5534, 5537, 5547 and 5552) either used in *naalbinding* or looped needle knitting.[269] All these bone needles are quite large at around 100 mm in length.

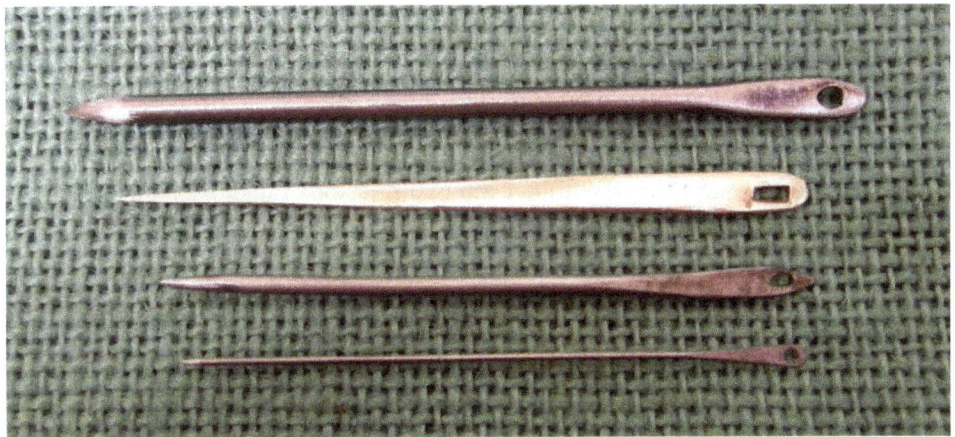

Figure 63 Reproduction iron and bronze needles

The needle finds from Flixborough show continual use of each type of material (bone, iron and non-ferrous) throughout the lifetime of the site with 7 copper alloy finds, 6 bone finds and 78 iron finds. From the available information it is clear to see that iron was the favoured needle-making material at every site.

---

[266] Ottaway, 1992
[267] Ottaway, 1992
[268] Ottaway, 1992
[269] Ottaway, 1992 p 1369

Flixborough bone and copper alloy finds (excavated complete)

Material	Find number	Date	Length
Copper alloy	2896	Mid 9th c.	55 mm
Copper alloy	2897	Mid-late 9th c.	52 mm
Copper alloy	2898	8th-9th c.	43 mm
Bone	2900	8th-9th c.	65 mm
Bone	2901	Mid-late 9th c.	93 mm
Bone	2903	8th-9th c.	70 mm
Bone	2904	10th-11th c.	63 mm
Bone	2905	Early-mid 9th c.	71 mm

Tablet Weaving

Tablet weaving has existed as a technique for millennia, but tablet weaving cards are rare due to their being made of wood. Only rare finds, such as the complete set and loom from the Oseberg (Norway) ship burial allow us a glimpse of those elusive textile tools.[270]

Evidence of the end-products of weaving is much more readily available than the equipment used to make them, but there are two finds of a tablet weaving card from the British Isles. The first is from the occupation levels at Bishopstone (East Sussex) of 8th - 11th c. date.[271] Find no. 89 is a bone weaving tablet, 33 x 30 mm by 2 mm thick with a round hole in each corner (one now broken). Secondly, find no. 6679 from Coppergate[272] (York) dated to 930-975AD is a square bone tablet some 27 x 24 mm in size with a hole in each corner and slight damage down one side.

The tablets were used in packs (up to several dozens in some cases) in the most complex braiding operations, so one card's casual loss or discard due to damage would not hinder the weaving process since spares would have been available.

Agricultural Tools

Food production is key to human survival, and the Anglo-Saxons in common with all peoples invested heavily in both time and tooling in this activity with most of the population in their pre-industrial society being directly involved in farming and its subsidiary industries.

---

[270] Walton-Rogers, 2007
[271] Thomas, 2010
[272] MacGregor, Mainman & Rogers, 1999

4 Tool Finds by Occupation

Land Clearance Tools

To grow crops one must first clear the land of existing vegetation, and the primary tool for this purpose is the bill or billhook. As is obvious the billhook differs from the bill in having a curved sickle-like blade for hooking round plant stems, while the bill is a long-handled slashing tool equally at home on the battlefield or on the land.

Bills and Billhooks

Known bill finds date exclusively to the latter part of the Anglo-Saxon period. From the 9th -10th c. Hurbuck Hoard (County Durham) comes a small bill. Two further similar finds from Flixborough (Lincolnshire) both came from unstratified contexts. They are recorded as finds 2361 and 2465, each of 260 mm tool length, and each is longer than the find from Hurbuck. One small and well-worn billhook now in the museum of Lewes Castle dating to the Anglo-Norman (11th – 12th c.) period indicates that both bill types were still in use at the end of the Anglo-Saxon period.

Figure 64 Reproductions of the Flixborough bill (above) and Lewess Castle billhook (below)

Fauchards

Two unusual billhooks (or 'fauchards' as they are otherwise called) are known. One is from a late 5th to mid-8th c. context in the Anglo-Saxon cemetery at Dover Buckland (Kent): the find from the male grave 437 consists of a long, thin socketed billhook, 334 mm in length with a side protrusion half way down the rear of the blade, forged in the shape of a miniature axehead. It has been suggested that this addition was an innovation introduced by the Romans, and research into Roman sickles and clearing tools does show this type of blade addition. Secondly, a fauchard of similar construction was excavated from grave 26 at Coddenham (Suffolk) of the 7th to early 8th c.[273] This example is much heavier than the Buckland

---

[273] Penn, 2011

find and with a protruding "finger" near the curved outer edge of the blade; it is slightly shorter than the Buckland example at 280 mm long Of interest is the inclusion of the tool in graves;. The Buckland grave was of high status, as shown by the inclusion of a sword, while the Coddenham grave was distinctly lower in status containing only a knife and belt buckle. The inclusion of the tool appears anomalous in both cases. The Dover example might conceivably have been used as a weapon, and warranted inclusion on that basis.

Tests with my reproduction tools have shown the bill to be a highly adaptable tool when used in woodland, being very effective at removing bracken and brambles.

Figure 65 Reproduction of the Dover Buckland fauchard

Ploughing Tools

Once an area of land has been cleared, it requires ploughing. In its simplest form the ard or plough is an iron-tipped wooden point dragged through the earth by oxen. In the case of the ard, the soil is displaced by a furrow while the plough has a separate element – the mouldboard – which turns the soil over.

Figure 66 Reproduction iron ploughshare

4 Tool Finds by Occupation

Ploughshares

The iron shoe is called a ploughshare and has one basic form: a triangulate plate with folded side-wings that grip the stock of the plough. From Anglo-Saxon contexts, several ploughshares are known. From the Nazeing (Essex) hoard comes a ploughshare of 176 mm long by 45 mm wide with winged tabs.[274] From Flixborough (Lincolnshire) is a find (no.2360) dated to an 8th to late 9th c. context, some 290 mm long and 123 mm wide.[275] From Thetford (Norfolk) comes a ploughshare similar in construction to the Flixborough find at 150 mm long and 65 mm wide.[276] There are other, less well-documented finds from St Neots (Cambridgeshire)[277] (of late Anglo-Saxon date) and Westley Waterless (Cambridgeshire) dated to 975-1066 AD.[278]

Finally there is a ploughshare from the occupation levels at Bishopstone[279] (East Sussex) (find no. 77 from hoard no. 5) some 172 mm long by 77 mm wide. All these ploughshare finds are of similar construction and size, and all are symmetrically constructed indicating that plough design was effectively standardised.

A plough with just a ploughshare is deemed to be a 'light plough', while a plough that features a coulter (a blade which cuts the soil in front of the ploughshare) is called a 'heavy plough' and it has always been assumed, based on the lack of direct evidence, that the Anglo-Saxons did not use them at least until the Anglo-Norman period (post-1066 AD). The heavy plough is shown in an 11th century manuscript (MS Cotton Tiberius B.V., part 1 now in the British Library), an Anglo-Saxon calendar showing "men ploughing the land".

Coulters

In Ælfric's *Colloquy on the Occupations*, dated to the 10th - 11th c., the ploughman refers to fitting the *culter* (Old English for coulter) before ploughing.[280] It is known that the Romans used the coulter with an example from Walthamstow (Essex) at 288 mm long (now in the British Museum). The assumption that the Anglo-Saxons did not use the coulter in the intervening period seems improbable, and two recent finds now clearly show that the coulter was in use throughout the Anglo-Saxon period. One is a 7th c. find by Dr Gabor Thomas and his team from the University of Reading made at Lyminge (Kent)[281] of an angled coulter some 500 mm long. The second is the discovery by Dr Kevin Leahy[282] of an angled coulter from Scraptoft (Leicestershire) again around 500 mm long and dated to around the 9th c. Both finds are so similar that they could have been made by the same smith!

---

[274] Morris, 1983
[275] Evans & Loveluck, 2009
[276] Goodall. 1984
[277] Addyman, 1983
[278] Fox, 1923
[279] Thomas, 2010
[280] Garmonsway, 1991
[281] Currently awaiting publication
[282] Leahy, 2013

4 Tool Finds by Occupation

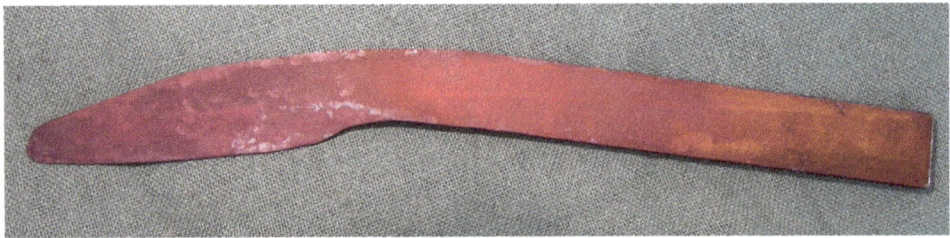

Figure 67 Reproduction of the Scraptoft coulter

These two finds, taken along with the Roman period evidence, suggest the continual use of the heavy plough throughout the Anglo-Saxon period. This does not mean, however, that the light plough would have been abandoned. The size of the area for ploughing and the availability of cattle dictate the size and type of plough used.

Mattocks

Ploughing produces soil of irregularly-shaped clumps which need breaking up, which is where the mattock comes into play. Following the plough, labourers (and children?) would break up the clods of earth with mattocks, a type of long-handled wooden mallet. A number of mattock finds exist from the Anglo-Saxon period, some from Coppergate (York) and especially the 9-10th century deposits from that site. The four finds are outlined below;

Find Number	Period	Head material
8971	Mid 9th - early 10th c.	Oak
8972	930/975 AD	Poplar/Aspen
8973	930/975 AD	Maple
8974	975-11th c.	Ash

Figure 68 Reproduction mattock made with an oak head and ashwood handle

The head is made separate from the shaft although the tool could be constructed in one piece. This would have disadvantages since the best qualities of shaft and head are rarely found in the same wood. A replaceable head makes repair and manufacture easier. All the mattocks from Coppergate conform to the same size range, the heads varying from 200 to 250 mm in length.

Mattocks can either be single- or double-ended (i.e. with one or two edged faces to the head), with one Coppergate example (find no.8972) being a well-constructed, double ended tool, while other examples from the site were more crudely fashioned. The Cotton Tiberius calendar[283] shows a scene for March with a man following the plough breaking a clod with a double-ended mattock similar to the Coppergate examples.

From the Anglo-Norman period onwards, it is understood that the heavy plough featured a mould-board - a shaped, curving board behind the ploughshare that turns the earth over into the characteristic long plough-lines that we see today. Since they were made of wood they do not survive, although it seems likely that they were a later addition to the heavy plough. Ploughs with mould-boards have an offset ploughshare, whereas all the known Anglo-Saxon examples are symmetrical. To some extent, the mould-board plough would obviate the need for teams of labourers with mattocks. Since there is evidence for the use of that tool, the mould-board may not have been employed. Nevertheless, there is evidence for the use of mouldboards as early as the 7th c. in Scotland (within a presumed Viking context) with the find of a wooden fragment of mouldboard and mould or plough-pebbles in situ. These are pebbles hammered into a hole in the mould board to act as a hard facing surface to protect the board from wear. On many agricultural sites, fieldwalking can reveal these pebbles in some numbers but it is of course difficult to date a worn pebble accurately. There are finds from datable contexts from the 9th c. at Jarlshof (Shetland).[284]

Drainage and Ditching Tools

Ploughed land requires drainage, which meant ditches dug by hand. They had a secondary but important function as boundary markers, and prevented cattle straying onto valuable crops in the fields. Three important tools were used for this purpose (and are still used today): the pick, shovel and spade. We are fortunate that a number of well-preserved examples are known from the Anglo-Saxon period.

Picks

From a 9th-10th c. context comes a pick from the Hurbuck hoard (County Durham), the only known find of such a tool from an Anglo-Saxon context.[285] It was formed from two strips of iron fire-welded along its length and round the eye forming a lenticular socket. Given that the rest of the hoard has an agricultural theme (axes, scythes, and a bill) it seems likely that the pick had an agricultural use as well.

---

[283] Cotton Tiberius B.V. - Anglo-Saxon calendar in the British Library.
[284] Hamilton, 1956
[285] Wilson, 1968

4 Tool Finds by Occupation

Figure 69 Reproduction of the Hurbuck pick

Shovels

The Anglo-Saxon shovel is a two-part composite device made of wood, designed for moving loose bulk material. The distinguishing feature between shovel and spade is that the shovel has an angled blade, whereas the spade's blade is in line with its shaft. The skilful construction of the Anglo-Saxon shovel combines light design with optimum strength; it is a flat shovel blade into which the handle slots by means of a square, angled recess, and the blade either secured with trenails, tied with cord or both. The advantage of a two-part shovel is (i) that it allows for an angled shovel blade for maximum material removal (as in modern steel on wooden shaft shovels) and (ii) the use of different woods, so that stronger and more hard-wearing oak can be used in the blade and springy ash can be used in the handle. We must not forget also the ease of manufacture and repair for shovels constructed from split wood, rather than hand-carved from a single piece of wood, thus allowing all but the most unskilled woodworkers to manufacture these tools.

Figure 70 Reproduction ashwood shovel of Morris's type C

4 Tool Finds by Occupation

Morris[286] identified five shovel-blade types (a to e) based on the rear blade-fixing profile, although with the construction of all handmade items there is always a variation in design form batch to batch. The Morris typography lists the distinct types, even though every individually made shovel would be a variation on a theme. All the shovels from Anglo-Saxon contexts show a good correlation in size which does not imply a standard template but more likely a known quantity of material that a man can easily move in a single shovelful.

The separate-bladed shovel enjoyed a long period of use, with examples ranging from the 10th c. to the 14th although it is likely that its introduction predates the 10th c. The shovels so far recovered from Britain during the Anglo-Saxon period number around fourteen examples (with more from later periods). There are seven examples from Dublin, all dated to the 11th c., with at least two of these featuring oak blades. An example from Exeter, again in oak, is dated to the 11th/12th c.[287] An 8-9th c. example was found on Moynagh Lough crannog, Co Meath (Ireland)[288] and the following well documented finds from Coppergate, York[289] are all in oak:

Find no.		Blade Type
9177	Coppergate watching brief[290]	B
8964	Coppergate, 930-975 AD	C
8965	Coppergate, 975-11th c.	C
8966	Coppergate, 975-11th c.	B
8967	Coppergate, 11-12th c.	?

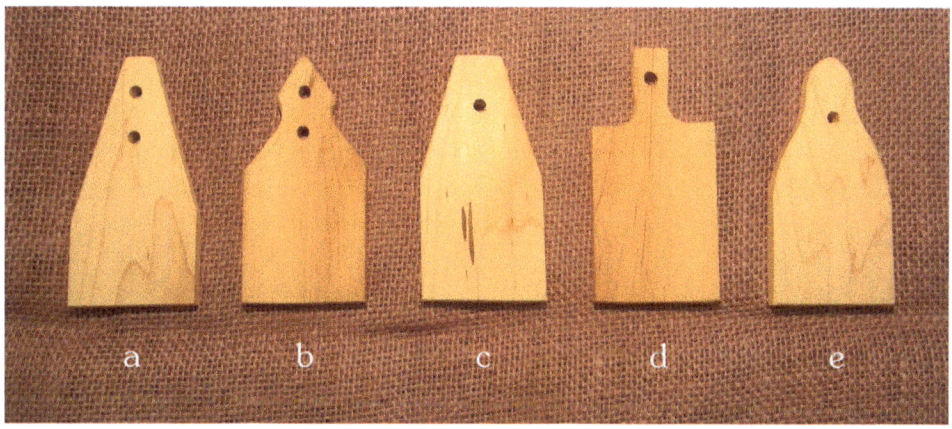

Figure 71 Reproductiion shovel-blade profiles in Morris's typology

---

[286] Morris, 1981
[287] Morris, 1981
[288] Bradley, 1982
[289] Morris, 2000
[290] Benson, 1906

4 Tool Finds by Occupation

Spades

Anglo-Saxon period spades were constructed from a single piece of wood with the cutting edge protected by a shoe or spade-iron, a U- or Y-section piece of iron formed round the blade tip and sides to protect the wood from damage. This "hardfacing" allows for a light, strong shovel with good wear resistance. Blade profiles, based on finds and manuscript illustrations, can according to Morris[291] be broadly placed in three categories: (i) rounded, (ii) triangulate and (iii) square/rectangular. It seems from the excavated evidence that the rounded profiles are a genuine Anglo-Saxon type, with the other two developing in the mid- to late medieval periods.

We are fortunate that a spade fragment in wood survives from the occupation levels at Coppergate (York), datable to the range 975-11th c. (the late Anglo-Scandinavian period). This find (no. 8969) is made from a single piece of oak with a rounded profile but missing its spade-iron. The blade and a short portion of the handle survive with an interesting feature of offset footrests on the back of the blade. This is a well-constructed design innovation, as it removes the plane of weakness at the blade/handle interface by offsetting the opposing corners. Generally only the spade-iron survives (in some cases only fragments) as can be seen from Coppergate (find no. 2748, Anglo-Scandinavian period) and more complete examples from Thetford (Norfolk),[292] Porchester Castle (Hampshire),[293] *Hamwic* - Southampton (Hampshire)[294] dated to the 8th - 9th c., Ufton Nervet (Berkshire)[295] and finally Sandton[296] (Kent) where the recovered iron had nail-hole lugs for fixing the shoe to the blade.

Figure 72 Reproduction of a wooden spade with iron shoe, Coppergate find 2748

---

[291] Morris, 2000
[292] Goodall, 1984
[293] Cunliffe. 1976
[294] Addyman & Hill, 1969
[295] Manning 1973-4
[296] Wilson, 1978

Harvesting Tools
The main harvesting tools are the scythe, sickle and reaping hook of which a number of examples have been recovered from Anglo-Saxon contexts.

Scythes
Scythe finds are limited to two major hoards: (i) the 9th -early 10th c. deposit at Hurbuck (County Durham) containing four scythe blades, three of which are complete; and (ii) an example in the Scraptoft Hoard (Leicestershire).[297] All the scythe finds are of roughly the same length (about 40 cm) with the tang forged at 90° to the blade, with a hook for fitting into the handle and tying on with twine.

Figure 73 Reproduction scythe with experimental ring locking mechanism

Two interesting points arise here. Firstly, the blades of the scythes are straight - unlike later scythes which have a curved blade; and secondly, the manuscript depiction (the Anglo-Saxon calendar discussed above, for August) shows the handles of the scythes as straight. The handle of a scythe is known as a "sned" and the traditional curved examples were introduced during the 12th century as an improvement on the Anglo-Saxon straight shaft.[298]

Sickles and Reaping Hooks
Sickles and reaping hooks have been grouped together for the purposes of discussion here: the main difference between the two is a matter of size, as both tools perform the same function. Sickle finds are rare in Anglo-Saxon contexts but some examples have been found, the most complete of which is from the 8th -11th c. occupation levels at Bishopstone (East Sussex).[299] This find (no. 76) is virtually complete, with a sweeping semi-circular blade some 200 mm long Other finds are generally

---
[297] Leahy, 2013
[298] Brigden, 1983
[299] Thomas, 2010

fragmentary with examples from Wensley (Yorkshire) dated to the 9th c.,[300] and a fragmentary find from the Anglo-Scandinavian levels at Coppergate, York (find 2749). The profile of the York fragment suggests a sickle with its tapered tip rather than a scythe which would usually have a rounded "nose" during the Anglo-Saxon period. There is also a fragmentary find of a sickle tip from the settlement area at Bloodmoor Hill, Carlton Coleville (Norfolk),[301] find no. 423, a well-formed piece with distal taper.

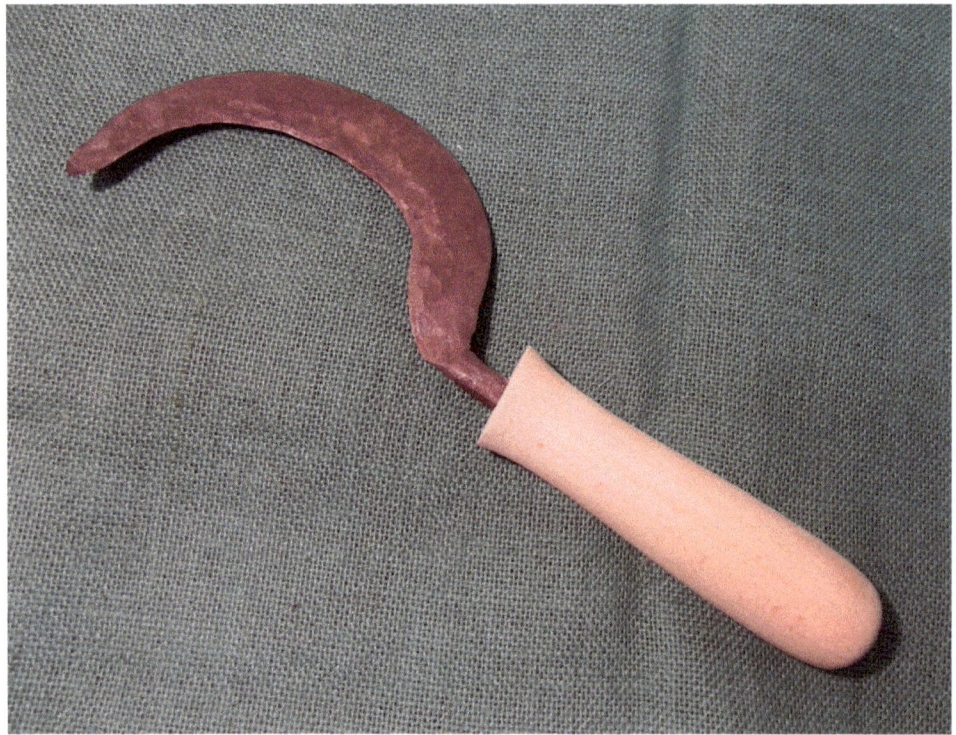

Figure 74 Reproduction sickle, Bishopstone-style

The reaping hook is a smaller version of the sickle, designed for lighter work. Generally the blade is no longer than 100 mm and is unusual in having a coiled external tang which is wound around the outside of the wooden handle. There are two examples: one from West Stow (Suffolk) dated to around 600 AD and a second find, now in Weston Park Museum, Sheffield, dated to the same period and recovered from a site in Derbyshire.

---

[300] Now in the British Museum, find no; AN472607001
[301] Lucy, Tipper & Dickens, 2009

4 Tool Finds by Occupation

Figure 75 Reproduction reaping hook based on a find from West Stow

Pitchforks

There is a supposed fragmentary find of a pitchfork tine from Coppergate[302] (York) dated to 930-975 AD, (find no. 2750). This item is heavy in construction and would be difficult to work with due to its weight being around 20 mm in diameter at its base and 20 cm long excluding the missing socket. Again we return to the 11th c. calendar (Cotton Tiberius, B. V. part 1, f.6v) and particularly the depiction for August which shows iron scythes, and a pitch fork. The pitchfork appears as a one-piece wooden tool and the iron scythe as a two-part tool.

Miscellaneous Tools

Not every tool fits easily into a category, either due to lack of finds or its unusual nature. Here we shall consider a list of such tools, some of which are only single finds and others belong to a fairly large group of artefacts. The list here is not exhaustive, as there is always the possibility of new classes of object being discovered.

Sharpening Steels

There are a number of possible sharpening steel finds from around Britain during the Anglo-Saxon period, with one notable example from grave 49 in the Anglo-Saxon cemetery at Winnall (Hampshire)[303] dated to the early Anglo-Saxon period. It is 14 cm long, wide-bladed at one end (about 2 cm) and tapering to a blunt point, found "parallel with and close to the knife". It is possible that the pointed end was a tang for inserting into a wooden handle, but no evidence for this remains. Of a more curious nature are the four finds from the Anglo-Saxon cemetery at Shrubland Hall Quarry, Coddenham (Suffolk) dating to the 7th to early 8th century, all to the same design of a flat section with a well-formed long tang also found in close proximity to their respective knives.[304] The shape of the Coddenham steels give rise to

---

[302] Ottaway,1992
[303] Meaney & Chadwick Hawkes, 1970
[304] Penn, 2011

a number of possibilities. In view of their well-formed, symmetrical shaping they are likely not to have had handles, indeed there is no evidence to suggest they did have. This gives rise to the possibility of alternative or dual uses: they could represent a new form of food pricker (an early precursor to the fork), they might be sharpening steels or they might be fire steels. All these suggestions are plausible and it is even possible that they served all three purposes. We can discount the possibility that they represent a form of pin-beater since graves 3, 5 and 48 are male with only one female find (grave 8). A find of a cast copper-alloy pin-beater was made in the Anglo-Saxon cemetery at Finglesham (Kent) (grave 180) that is effectively of the same design as the iron finds from Coddenham!.

Figure 76 Reproduction sharpening steels: Winall (above) Coddenham (below)

Further sharpening steel finds were made at Finglesham, e.g. from grave 133 (male) comes a steel with the remnants of an antler or bone handle, of rather crude workmanship and there are further examples from graves 129B (male) and 150 (female) that conform to the design of the Winnall II find, being of a tapered spatulate profile.[305] Lastly, a steel of unusual design was discovered in the Anglian burial site at Wigber Low (Derbyshire), (find 1813) a spatulate tool with one pointed (possibly a tang) and one curled end.[306] This tool could either be a sharpening steel, a fire steel or an ornate pricker; it was found in a male grave.

---

[305] Meaney & Chadwick Hawkes, 1970
[306] Collis, 1983

4 Tool Finds by Occupation

Bread Peels

Figure 77 Reproduction of a wooden bread peel from Coppergate (find no.8923)

From the Coppergate excavations in York, find no.8922 dating to the second half of the 9th c. is that of a bread peel, manufactured from a single piece of alder wood with a flat blade 12 cm wide x 16 cm long and with rounded and well-used corners, marked with a circle and cross which may be an amuletic protective mark for the bread.[307] This tool was used to place the risen dough in the bread oven to bake, and for its removal when ready.

Flesh Hooks and Forks

From Coppergate (York)[308] comes a flesh fork fragment (find no.2990) and also a socketed fork (find no.2989) some 12 cm long (including socket) dated to the Anglo-Scandinavian period. From the Lloyds Bank site[309] in the same city comes an unusual flesh fork (find no.428) - a three pronged fork hafted at 90 degrees to the handle, some 71mm long by 43mm wide.

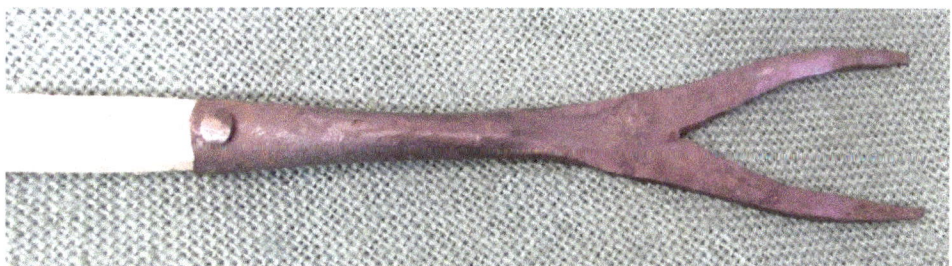

Figure 78 Reproduction of the Coppergate fork, find no.2989

---

[307] Morris, 2000
[308] Ottaway, 1992
[309] MacGregor, 1982

Dry Rakes

Figure 79 Reproduction dry rake with metal shoe in place

Dry rakes were used for the moving of bulk semi-liquid or dry material, such as for drying seed on a hot floor or for use in the tanning process. From Anglo-Scandinavian York comes a dry rake (no. 8976)[310] from Coppergate dated to 930-975 AD. It is possible that this rake-head also had an iron shoe which was removed before the rake-head was discarded. The damage to the wooden head suggests it was used in a hot environment, such as raking coals in a fire or oven. This is the first in a series of dry rake-heads recovered from the Coppergate excavation spreading from the Anglo-Scandinavian into the mid- to late medieval periods.

Mill Picks

The mill pick is a cigar-shaped piece of iron or steel set into a wooden handle (called a 'thrift') which was used to work stone, usually in the manufacture of quern stones. There are two probable mill pick finds from Britain; one is from Coppergate,[311] (York) (find no. 2271) at 78 mm long and the other from Bloodmoor Hill, Carlton Coleville (Suffolk) (find 336) 53 mm long.[312]

Figure 80 Reproduction Coppergate mill pick in a conjectural handle

---

[310] Morris, 2000
[311] Ottaway, 1992
[312] Lucy, Tipper & Dickens, 2009

4 Tool Finds by Occupation

Fishing Tackle

Fish Spear

Fish was an important part of the Anglo-Saxon diet as most settlements were close to a stream, river or estuary. This is reflected in the number of fish-related tools and pieces of equipment recovered by excavation. Of all the finds, probably the most surprising item is the fish spear from the Nazeing hoard (Essex) (figure 2).[313] Although the hoard was probably deposited in the 10th c. it also contains artefacts from much earlier in the Anglo-Saxon period, so an exact date for the spear is impossible to determine - it could even be Late Roman. The tool is in tridentine form with three barbed tines, each 87 mm long with a total length of the spear around 211 mm including the socket. So far, this find is unique in an Anglo-Saxon context from Britain.

Fish Hooks

Listed below are the fish hook finds from a number of settlement sites: Coppergate and Fishergate (York), Bloodmoor Hill, Carlton Coleville (Suffolk) and Flixborough (Lincolnshire). In many cases, the recovered fish hooks are fragmentary so the sizes listed relate to the existing finds and not the original lengths.

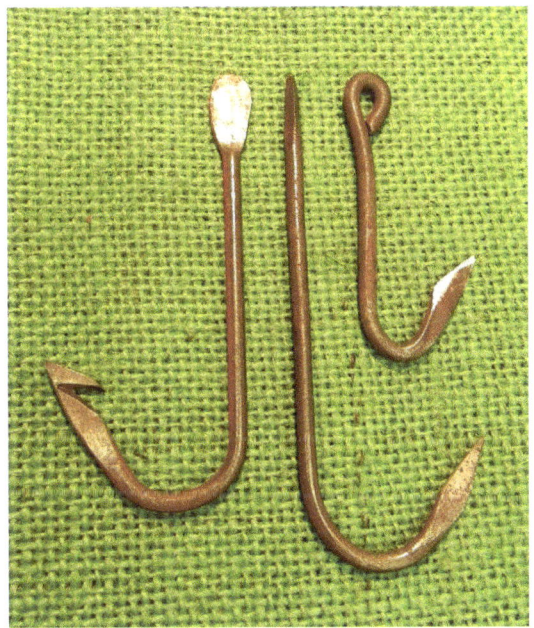

Figure 81 Three reproduction fish hooks - barbed, pointed and wedge

---

[313] Morris, 1983

4 Tool Finds by Occupation

Fish hooks from four settlement sites

Find spot	Find reference	Head: eye, spade or taper	Tip: point barbed or wedge	Length mm	Date
Coppergate	2991	E	B	54	Anglo-Scan
	2892	S		54	Anglo-Scan
	2993	E		56	Anglo-Scan
	2995	S	B	56	Anglo-Scan
	2994	S			Anglo-Scan
	2996		B		Anglo-Scan
	2997		B		Anglo-Scan
Fishergate	5038		B	49.2	Pre 8th c.
	5039		B	25.1	8th-9th c.
	5041		B		11th-12th c.
Bloodmoor Hill	424		P	14	6th-8th c.
	425	S		18	6th-8th c.
	426		P	20	6th-8th c.
	427			24	6th-8th c.
	428		P	25	6th-8th c.
	429		P	26	6th-8th c.
	430			14	6th-8th c.
	431			18	6th-8th c.
	432		P	21	6th-8th c.
Flixborough	2405	T	P	16	10th -11th c.
	2406	T	P	21	Mid 9th c.
	2407	T	P	21	10th -11th c.
	2408	T	P	16	10th -11th c.
	2409	T	P	16	Late 9th c.
	2410	T	P	19	10th -11th c.
	2411	T	P	30	Late 9th c.
	2412	T	P	18	unstratified
	2413	T	W	21	10th -11th c.
	2414	T	W	23	10th -11th c.
	2415	T	W	33	unstratified
	2416	T	W	23	unstratified
	2417	T		18	8th -9th c.
	2418	T		17	10th -11th c.
	2419	T		20	10th -11th c.
	2420	T		15	10th -11th c.
	2421	T		17	unstratified
	2422	T		38	unstratified

Fish hooks have one of two principal head-types for securing the thread - either a rolled eye or a spade head; the latter rarely survives, as has been found from reconstructions where the forged head is very weak. A third type of head is apparently so far unique to the Flixborough site in that it has a tapered shaft. Some of the recovered finds have mineralised wood attachments, leading to the suggestion that these fish hooks were set in wooden blocks and floated on the water, perhaps roped together in bundles.

Net Weights

The final fishing related item considered here are net weights, which are technically not a tool but rather fishing equipment. They are included here for completeness as they form part of a fishing net.

Netting weights or sinkers have been recovered from around Britain, usually cast in lead or lead alloy. They can be broadly classed into barrel, cylindrical and hooped profiles. From Flixborough[314] come 9 barrelled, 11 cylindrical and 5 hooped, all made from lead and simply folded or wrapped round the net. From Fishergate[315] (York) come three lead sinkers (find 5477-9) from the 8th -9th c. and a further four from the 10th - 12th c. levels (finds 5480-3) (as well as stone sinkers) and one find from the 8th - 9th c. levels (find 4459) and two (4460-1) from the 10th-12th c. levels. Dating sinkers can be difficult as they have no diagnostic features except the context in which they were found. It is possible that some of the Flixborough sinkers are residual Iron Age finds.

Pottery stamps

Pottery stamps can be made out of wood, bone or antler - or in rare cases metal. Wood does not survive archaeologically but we have a few bone and antler examples.

From Caudle Common, Eriswell (Suffolk) comes an antler tine with a motif of three concentric rings, nominally 11.5 mm diameter.[316] From Winchester comes an antler tine with a motif of a spoked-wheel type marked in eight segments; it is now in Winchester Museum.[317] Both finds are dated to the Anglo-Saxon period. On the online database of the Portable Antiquity Scheme are records of three stamps, all dated to the Anglo-Saxon period.[318] They are:

NMS-369 EB4, a copper alloy stamp, 7 mm in diameter with an incised quartered circle, from Foulsham (Norfolk) dated to 410-720 AD.

LIN-6C7948, a 6.5 mm diameter early medieval copper-alloy stamp from Lincolnshire, with both ends marked with a quartered circle, each quarter containing a dot; the find is currently unvalidated.

LEIC-B7B493 from Leicestershire dated to the early medieval period (Anglo-Saxon) found at the Melbourne Roman town site, decorated with an incised quartered round stamp on an antler tine.

---

[314] Evans & Loveluck, 2009
[315] Rogers, 1993
[316] West, 1998, p156
[317] Reference WINLM:SXS74-80
[318] In this book, a section has been given over to the tool finds of the PAS but it is prudent to list the stamp finds here separately.

5 Tool Signatures

Not every tool survives as a buried artefact, most exist above ground until they fail and are replaced. Over time the types of toll used by the Anglo-Saxons have transmute into the tools we use today. Sometimes the evidence of their existence comprises nothing more than a word in the language or the characteristic marks they leave on the workpiece.

"Absence of evidence is not evidence of absence" as the archaeologists' dictum goes – but can absence of evidence really be taken to allow the possibility of presence? How far can we fairly take the argument that such-and-such a tool may have been in use, even though there is no hard evidence for it? To illustrate this point we shall consider the pump drill and the bow drill: both these tools have the same design feature in that they create reciprocating rotary motion, both are hand-powered tools and as such have limited force so the holes they can drill or auger marks they can make are generally small.

We know that many ancient societies, including the Egyptians and Romans, had both drill types as paintings and other representations of the objects survive, but no such illustrative evidence exists from the Anglo-Saxon period in Britain or elsewhere in northern Europe. To reach a reasoned conclusion as to whether these tools were in existence in Anglo-Saxon England, we have to compile a research dossier and then review the evidence fairly, not giving too much weight to any single datum. Here, both language and physical evidence combine to provide the a case.

We shall first consider as an example the pump drill. The earliest depiction of a pump drill is from the *Book of Games* (*Libero de los Juegos*) part of the folio of work on the manufacture of games commissioned by the then King of Castille, Alphonso X, and dated to 1293 AD. In shape and construction it is similar to Roman and Egyptian examples. In Old Norse (Old Icelandic) there are references to a 'fire drill' (*bragð-alr*) or in modern English a "twirling awl".[319] From this linguistic evidence we can assume the use of a reciprocating drill of some sort. Both pump and bow drills might be described as twirling awls, i.e. boring devices characterised by a sudden motion. Physical evidence for such drills comes from bone and antler work and also metalwork finds. Many Anglo-Saxon artefacts are decorated with ring-and-dot motifs with both single- and double-ring designs, and it is likely that either the pump or bow drill were responsible for their production. It is possible to produce the ring-and-dot with hand-twist awls, but it is slow and not as clean in execution as the pump drill. Using a variant form of ring-and-dot tip, beads can be made by drilling each side of a bone plate until there is a break. Find no. 7956 from the 9th c. levels at the Bedern Foundry[320] in York is clearly such a piece of bone waste from the drilling operation, consisting of eight smoothly augered holes in a plate.

---

[319] Cleasby & Vigfússon, 1874, s.v. *bragð* – the basic sense is sudden or short-lived motion.
[320] MacGregor, Mainman & Rogers, 1999

5 Tool Signatures

From the Anglo-Saxon cemetery at Castledyke South[321] (Humberside) (grave 163) comes a find of a quartz crystal bead with a neatly drilled hole through the centre, nominally 2 mm in diameter, obviously executed with a drill.[322]

My reconstructive research in the drilling of mild steel plate using the pump drill shows the suitability of the tool for the job, with a neat 3 mm hole drilled through a 3mm thick mild steel plate in around 20 minutes - fast technology for the 7th century! This application of the bow and pump drill on metal artefacts is evidenced on a number of examples recovered from Flixborough[323] (Lincolnshire) (600-1000AD), most notably in the case of pin find no. 527 (RF2838) which has three drilled ring-marks on the head using a metal version of the ring-and-dot auger used on bone. This points to the use of the reciprocating drill - either pump or bow.

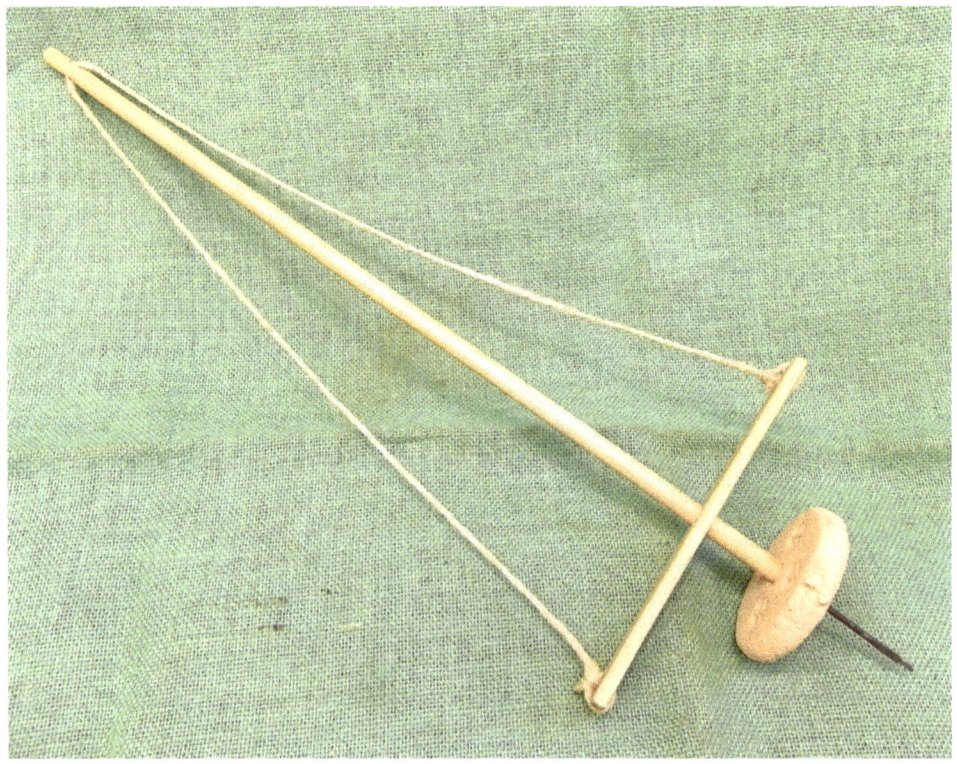

Figure 82 Reprodction of a pump drill

---

[321] Drinkall & Foreman, 1998, p382
[322] It might be argued that such a bead was manufactured in the Mediterranean area where quartz beads are a common dress item, but the bone plate from York (no.7956) clearly shows beadmaking on the site.
[323] Evans & Loveluck, 2009

6 The Portable Antiquities Scheme

The Portable Antiquities Scheme (PAS) allows members of the public to register casual archaeological finds from any period up to the modern. The purpose of the scheme is to catalogue these finds in an online database (accessible at www.finds.org.uk) the advantage which is that hitherto unknown sites of archaeological interest may present themselves through concentrations of finds, artefact types considered rare based on museum acquisitions may prove to have been common and all the information collated in a structured and queriable database adds to our knowledge of all periods. In the PAS online catalogue are a number of tool finds, but dating such finds is a difficult task as casual losses often defy seriation and have no useful context, especially when in isolation displaced in the topsoil. The allocated date-ranges for the finds are often deliberately vague, especially so with tools whose form generally only changes in Darwinian "jumps" due to new materials or manufacturing techniques. Listed below are some PAS-recorded objects identified as tools that have a diagnostically or acceptably Anglo-Saxon or Anglo-Norman shape.

Tool	Date Range (AD)	P.A.S.reference
Axe	700-1100	NLM-A77612
Axe	750-950	NLM-6CB595
Axe	950-1100	BUC-B7ACE2
Axe	500-1500	LEIC-FFC3A4
Axe	1000-1500	HESH-650301
Axe	900-1200	BERK-23A863
Axe	Early medieval	KENT-9C76D4
Adze	8th-12th c.	LANCUM-083FD6
Cold chisel	700-1100	NLM96
Scythe	8th-12th c.	LANCUM-F82IA3
Scythe	8th-12th c.	LANCUM-F80DD5
Scythe	8th-12th c.	LANCUM-F7CIB2
Scythe	8th-12th c.	LANCUM-F798A6
Awl	400-1100	SWYOR-2B5DA5
Awl	Early medieval	LVPL-BE43D4
Awl	600-800	CAM-05BA36

The PAS finds of scythe blades are very similar to the scythe find from the Scraptoft hoard[324] which has a safely dateable Anglo-Saxon context. In the main the recovered axeheads also conform to known Anglo-Saxon types.

Part of the value of the PAS is that it is continually expanding, allowing further associations between objects and improving the accuracy with which such finds may be identified.

---

[324] Leahy, 2013

7 Conclusion

I hope to have shown in the previous chapters that the range of tools available during the Anglo-Saxon period was adapted to their particular circumstances. We have looked at the gross earth-moving and agricultural tools wielded with great force by farmworkers, and the delicate and ephemeral textile tools used by high-status females in the weaving sheds and bowers where so much fine needlework took place.

As the photographs demonstrate, I have sought to recreate many of the tool types and even individual examples. Through such practical study, I have come to understand something of the workshop practices and techniques used by those craftsmen over several centuries. As I mentioned in the Introduction, the Anglo-Saxon do not seem to have introduced any new types of tool to the world but they perfected the use of most of the tools they already had.

Appendix 1

Stamp Forms in Non-Ferrous Metal

Stamping metalwork for decorative effect predates the Anglo-Saxon period by millennia. It seems likely that metal-stamping is a development of pottery stamping, which finds its roots deep in the Neolithic period. In Anglo-Saxon contexts there are some eighty or so main stamp types listed below but it must be remembered that there are numerous slight variations on patterns. Any stamp may have had a limited product run. The patterns here are derived from archaeological line drawings and some of the stamps are conjectural, indeed some stamps may be composite, made up of separate parts likely to be two stamps applied separately.

The reconstructions given here are approximations based on the original drawings and therefore are slightly stylised renditions of the original stamps within the limitations of computer-generated images and my attempts at replication. Anglo-Saxon stamp application is (to say the least) somewhat variable, ranging from the beautifully executed to what we may suspect to be drunken fumblings.

It could be said that the idea of stamping exceeds the execution: this is one of the contradictions of the Anglo-Saxon period where we may find well-crafted treasures side by side with badly decorated scrap. Possession and display of decorative metalwork marked its owner as to some extent removed from the mundane and the unfree classes. Stamps do seem to show regional or local tastes, in that some cemeteries are bereft of punchwork whilst others are richly adorned with numerous stamp motifs. Little research has been carried out on the meaning associated with particular stamps or stamp sets.[325] From the examples given here (which are selective, not exhaustive) it can be seen that most stamp designs can be used on many different items and that triangulate stamps are favoured above all others in so far as they form the basis for the most numerous designs. The black areas on the stamps indicate indented areas, whereas on some of the line stamps it could be that the lines were indented into the stamp to leave a raised shape in the punched metal with the corners of the punch domed to show no indentation. It must also be noted that these are derived from the archaeologists' original line drawings and as a result can be open to interpretation.

The size of some of these stamps is interesting in that even those of complex design can be as little as 1 mm in width/height and, as my own experiments have shown, would have required no great level of skill to produce but a good level of magnification. One candidate for a means of optical magnification would be some sort of polished quartz crystal but it is debatable whether true lenses could have been produced. Alternatively (as my work demonstrates) a number of attempts at making a punch would eventually lead to a serviceable tool.

---

[325] Cf. Richards, 1987

Stamp Forms in Non-Ferrous Metals

Each of the stamps or punchmarks listed below has been given a reference number with an example of where the punchmark was found, including findspot (usually a cemetery) followed by the grave number and find number, and lastly the class of item upon which it was found. Many of the stamps have been found in a number of locations but only one find spot is listed for the sake of brevity (which does not imply a unique use in that cemetery). Many of these stamps have widespread use on many items and in several cemetery locations. The lists given here are broadly categorised into four main groupings - triangles, circles, curves and squares.

Appendix 1

Stamp	Cemetery	Grave/find	Item
C1	Eriswell	25/2	Cruciform Brooch
C2	Morning Thorpe	38/C	Strap End
C3	Morning Thorpe	7/Ci	Plate
C4	Morning Thorpe	288/E	Square Headed Brooch
C11	Empingham	4a/1	Annular Brooch
C12	Butlers Field	92/7	Strip
C13	Morning Thorpe	299/P	Annular Brooch
C14	Morning Thorpe	288/E	Square Headed Brooch
C15	Bergh Apton	62/Bii	Spangle
C16	Empingham	61/4	Wrist clasp
C17	Morning Thorpe	342/M	Square Headed Brooch
C18	Spong Hill	1064	Plate
C19	Oakley	118/10	Spangle
C20	Worthy Park	58/6	Sheet
C21	Empingham	50/1	Cruciform Brooch
C22	Morning Thorpe	397/Li	Girdle Hanger
C23	Dover Buckland	250/a	Gold Bracteate
C24	Empingham	40/1	Annular Brooch
C25	Empingham	6/7	Wrist Clasp
C26	Empingham	50/1	Cruciform Brooch
C27	Butlers Field	88/5	Strip
C28	Worthy Park	50/3	Tweezers
C29	Springfield Lyons	4988/1	Cruciform Brooch
C30	Morning Thorpe	97/Bi	Wrist Clasp

Stamp Forms in Non-Ferrous Metals

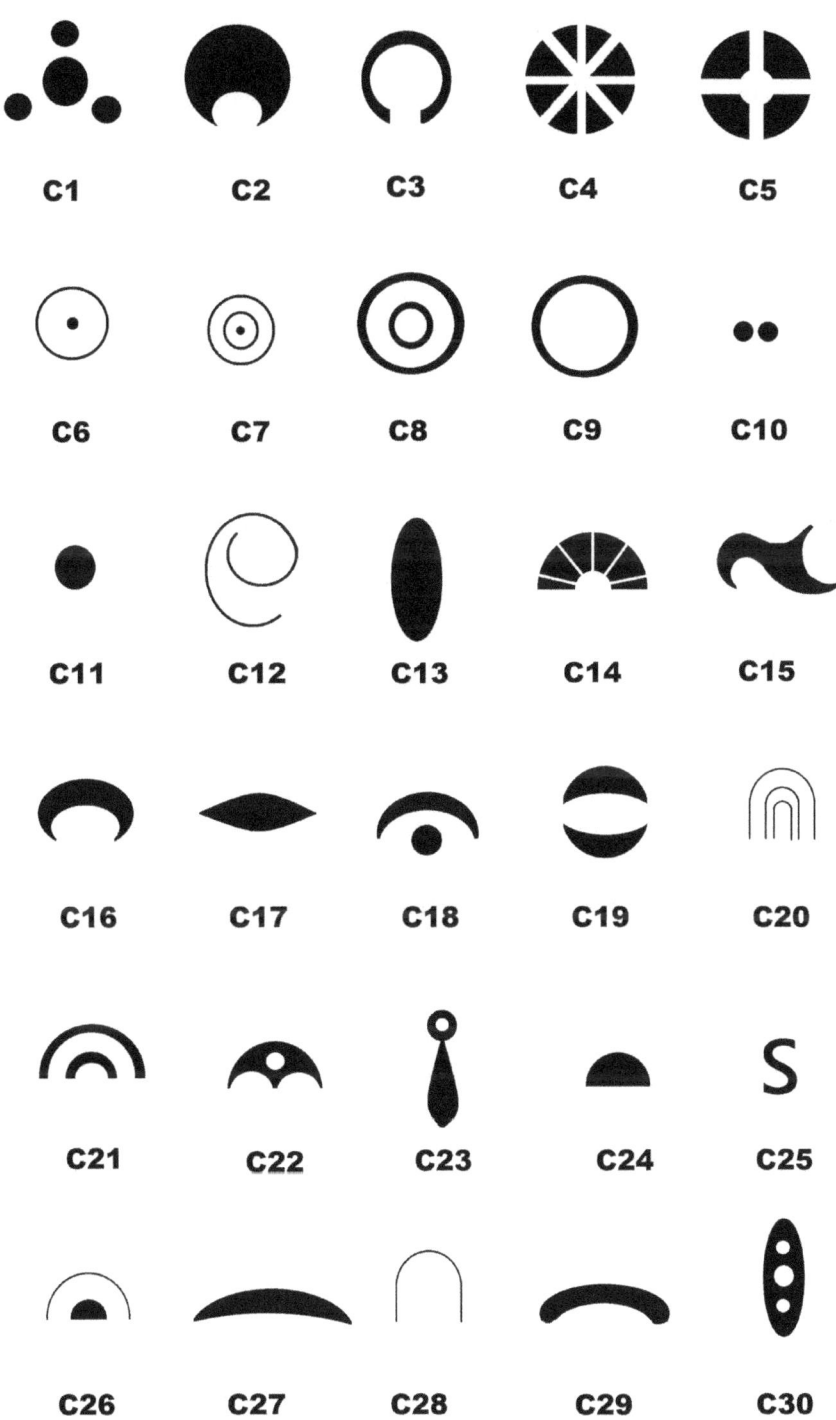

Appendix 1

Stamp	Cemetery	Grave/find	Item
S1	Blacknall Field	95/1	Small Long brooch
S2	Bergh Apton	21/C	Disc Brooch
S3	Blacknall Field	31/3	Square headed brooch
S4	Bergh Apton	34/Ai	Strap End
S5	Blacknall Field	95/1	Small Long Brooch
S6	Bergh Apton	29/Hi	Buckle Plate
S7	Empingham	40/14	Strap End
S8	Springfield Lyons	2545/1	Strap End
S5	Blacknall Field	95/1	Small Long Brooch
S6	Bergh Apton	29/Hi	Buckle Plate
S7	Empingham	40/14	Strap End
S8	Springfield Lyons	2545/1	Strap End
S9	Morning Thorpe	253/K	Girdle Hanger
S10	Morning Thorpe	35/Di	Cruciform Brooch
S11	Bloodmoor Hill	Fig 16/9	Cruciform Brooch
T1	Empingham	42/5	Wrist Clasp
T2	Dover Buckland	65/8	Tweezers
T3	Bergh Apton	7/H	Square Headed Brooch
T4	Morning Thorpe	30/Gi	Wrist Clasp
T5	Eriswell	39/5.1	Annular Brooch
T6	Worthy Park	77/1	Quoit Brooch
T7	Springfield Lyons	2906/1	Disc Brooch
T8	Worthy Park	10/4	Silver Ring
T9	Empingham	52/1	Cruciform Brooch
T10	Morning Thorpe	322/Ei	Disc Brooch
T11	Freckenham	46/10.1	Horned Small-Long Brooch
T12	Morning Thorpe	322/Ei	Disc Brooch
T13	Morning Thorpe	369/K	Annular Brooch
T14	Exning	44/1	Cruciform Brooch

Stamp Forms in Non-Ferrous Metals

Appendix 1

Stamp	Cemetery	Grave/find	Item
T15	Empingham	37/2	Annular brooch
T16	Eriswell	39/2	Annular Brooch
T17	Empingham	90/1	Disc Brooch
T18	Hindersley	48/16	Girdle Hanger
T19	Morning Thorpe	131/B	Annular Brooch
T20	Empingham	94/4	Disc Brooch
T21	Empingham	85B/9	Girdle Hanger
T22	Ipswich	59/1	Square Headed Brooch
T23	Empingham	40/20	Belt Buckle
T24	Morning Thorpe	288/E	Square Headed Brooch
T25	Morning Thorpe	137/Fi	Wrist Clasp
T26	Springfield Lyons	6573/4	Casting
T27	Exning	41/4	Cruciform Brooch
T28	Tuddenham	130/3	Cruciform Brooch
T29	Empingham	16A/1	Swastika brooch
T30	Bury St Edmunds	Fig 15/3	Square Headed Brooch
T31	Worthy Park	10/5	Silver ring
T32	Ipswich	64/2	Square Headed Brooch
T33	Empingham	24/5	Wrist Clasp
T34	Ipswich	61/1	Square Headed Brooch
T35	Empingham	42/8	Wrist Clasp
T36	Private Collection	136/2	Cruciform Brooch
T37	Empingham	15/2	Wrist Clasp

Stamp Forms in Non-Ferrous Metals

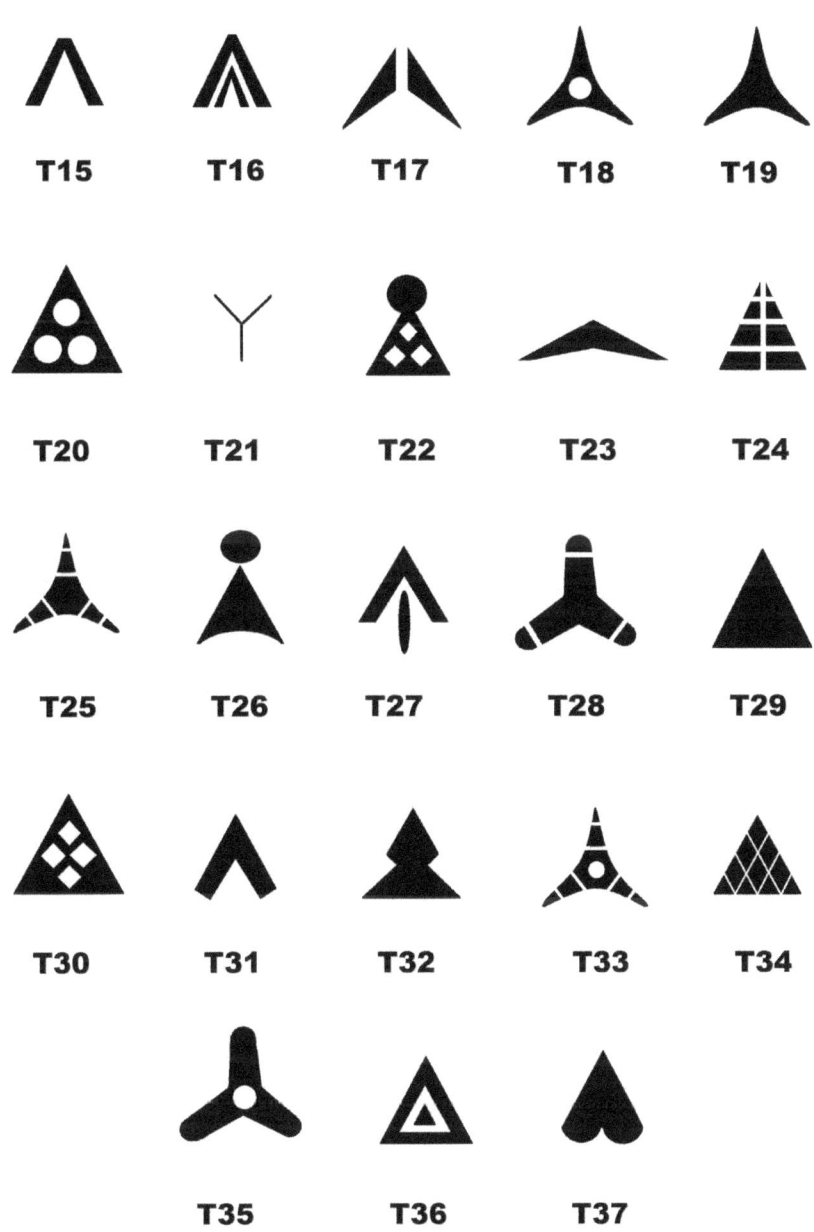

Appendix 2
Anglo-Saxon Tool Ferrules

Figure 83 Reproduction ferrules
left: Scraptoft hoard, right: Coppergate find no.2731

Tool ferrule finds are rare in any Anglo-Saxon context. Most iron tools which originally had a handle are either recovered with no evidence of the wood or may even have been deposited without the handle. This leaves us with the problem of deciding whether handles routinely had ferrules to stop the wood splitting or whether ferrules were considered unnecessary.

The two ferrule finds discussed below suggest that, on the whole, wooden handles were not provided with ferrules. Finds of tools with ferrules are exceptional.

The first example of a ferrule is from Anglo-Scandinavian Coppergate (York) dated to the 9th - 10th c. (find no.2731)[326] which was found in situ with an awl. The ferrule's construction was simple, being just a strip of iron folded into a circle with a nail through each end pinned into the wood. This indicates that the ferrule was wrapped round the wood before nailing, whereas a riveted ring shows that it was hammered on after fixing. In either case, the shank of the awl was then inserted into the handle. The second ferrule comes from the Scraptoft hoard[327] and is of a rather cunning construction - a thin, triangular strip of iron with a slot punched into the wider end. When the strip was rolled into a circle, the pointed end of the triangle fitted into the slot and was folded back upon itself to lock the ring which was then hammered onto the handle prior to inserting the tool's tang.

---

[326] Ottaway, 1992
[327] Leahy, 2013

Appendix 3
Anglo-Saxon Tools Wordlist

This list is by no means complete but includes the Old English names for some common tools and their equivalent modern English form (listed first). For those wishing to learn more about Old English (OE), I recommend the many excellent works of Steve Pollington. As an aid to pronunciation the following Old English letters and combinations are shown with their modern English equivalents.

OE letter	modern	OE word	meaning
Ð, ð	'th'	bæð	bath
sc	'sh'	sceð	sheath
Þ, þ	'th'	þorn	thorn
ge-	'ye-'	gear	year
Æ, æ	'a'	fæst	fast, firm
cg	'dg'	ecg	edge
-ig	'-y'	cræftig	crafty, skilful

Adze	adesa	Ladder	hlædder
Awl	æl	Mallet	slic
Axe	æcs	Mattock	becca
Bellows	blæstbelg	Nail	nægl, sceað
Blade	iren	Needle	nædl
Chisel	brædisen	Pitchfork	forcel
Clothshears	hræglsceara	Plane	locor, scafa
Coulter	culter	Rake	egðe
Drill	bor	Razor	scearseax
File	feol	Saw	sagu
Fish hook	angil	Scissors	scearra
Fork	forca	Shovel	scofl
Hammer	hamor, slecg	Sledgehammer	slecg
Handle	hlyfe	Spade	delfisen, spadu
Hatchet	wudubil	Stone chisel	cweornbil
Hoe	tyrfhag	Tongs	getang
Knife	seax		

Bibliography

Addyman, P.V. *Late Saxon Settlement in the St Neots Area II; the Little Paxton Settlement and Enclosure.*
Proceedings of the Cambridge Antiquarian Society, 1969

- *Late Saxon Settlement in the St Neots Area.* Proceedings of the Cambridge Antiquarian Society. 1973

Addyman, P.V. & Hill, D.H. *Saxon Southampton- a review of the Evidence, Part 2.*
Proceedings of the Hampshire Field Club & Archaeology Society vol.26, 1969

Akerman ,J.Y. *Remains of Pagan Saxondom,* London, 1855

Alexander, M. *Introduction to Heritage Assets: Mills,* May 2011

Angersen, H.H. & Madsen, H.J. *Byudgravening Ved Århuskatendralskule,* Kuml, 1985

Annable, F.K. & Eagles, B.N. *The Anglo-Saxon Cemetery at Blacknall Field, Pewsey, Wiltshire,* Devizes, 2010

Arbman, H. *Birka 1, Die Gräber Tafeln,* Uppsala, 1940

Arwidssen, G. *Valsgärde 6, Alta Musei Antiquitatum Septentrion Alium Regiace.* Universitatis Upsaliensis, Uppsala, 1942

- . *Die Gräberfunde Von Valsgärde III; Valsgärde 7.* Uppsala, 1977

Arwidsson, G. & Berg, G. *The Mästermyr Find,* Stockholm, 1983

Benson,G. *Notes on an Excavation at the Corner of Castlegate & Coppergate,* Yorkshire Philosophical Society Annual Report, vol. 72-6, 1906

Biddle, M. (Ed) *Objects and Economy in Medieval Winchester,* Oxford, 1990

Bindheim, C. *Smedgraven fra Bygland i Morgendal,* Viking 26, 1962

Blockley, K. Blockley, M. Blockley, P., Frere, S.S. & Stow, S. *Excavations in the Marlowe Car Park and Surrounding Areas.* Canterbury archaeological Trust, Canterbury, 1995

Boyle, A. Jennings, B. Milcs, D & Palmer, S. *The Anglo-Saxon Cemetery at Butlers Field, Lechlade, Gloucestershire,* Oxford, 1988

Bradley, J. *Excavations at Moynagh Lough, County Meath,* in The Journal of the Royal Society Of Antiquaries of Ireland, vol. 121, 1991

Brigden, R. *Agriculture and Tools.* Shire Publications, 1983

Brisbane, M. & Hather, J. (editors). *Wood Use in Medieval Novgorod.* Oxford, 2007

Bulleid, A. & Grey, H. *The Glastonbury Lake Village.* The Glastonbury Antiquarian Society, 1911

Bibliography

Carver, M.O.H. (ed) *The Age of Sutton Hoo; The Seventh Century in North Western Europe.* Woodbridge, 1992

- *An Iona of the East; The Early Medieval monastery at Portmahomach, Tarbat Ness.* Medieval Archaeology, vol.48, 2004

Chadwick Hawkes, S. & Grainger, G. *The Anglo-Saxon Cemetery at Finglesham, Kent.* Oxford, 2006

Cleasby, R. & Vigfusson, G. *An Icelandic English Dictionary* Oxford, Clarendon, 1957

Coatsworth, E & Pinder, M. *The Art of the Anglo-Saxon Goldsmith; Fine Metalwork in Anglo-Saxon England; Its Practice and Practitioners.* Woodbridge, 2002

Collis, J. *Wigber Low Derbyshire; A Bronze Age and Anglian Burial Site in the White Peak,* Sheffield, 1983

Cunliffe, B.W. *Excavations at Porchester Castle II; Saxon.* Research Committee of the Society of Antiquaries of London, London, 1976

Davies, S.M. Bojko, A.M. Crowfoot, E. Harding, P. & Henderson, J. *The Excavation of an Anglo-Saxon Cemetery (and some Prehistoric Pits) at Charlton Plantation near Downtown in Wiltshire,* Archaeological and Natural History Magazine, Volume 79, Devizes, 1984

Decaens, J. *Un Nouveau Cimitiere du Haut Moyen Age en Normandie: Herouvillette (Calvados).* Archaeologie Médiévale I, 1971

Dent, J. *Skerne,* Current Archaeology 91, 1984

Dobat, A.S. *Werkzeuge aus Kaiserzeitlichen Heeresausrüstungsopfern.* Aarhus University Press, Aarhus, Denmark, 2008

Drinkall, G. & Foreman, M. *The Anglo-Saxon Cemetery at Castledyke South, Barton on Humber.* Sheffield Excavation Report no 6, Sheffield, 1998

Dunning, G.C. *The Anglo-Saxon Plane from Sarre.* Archaeologia Cantiana 63, 1959

Eagles, B.N. & Evison, V.I. *Excavations at Harrold, Bedfordshire, 1951-3.* Bedfordshire Archaeological Journal 5, 1970

Ellis, S.E. *The Petrography and Provenance of Anglo-Saxon and Medieval English Hone Stones with Notes on other Hones.* Bull, British Museum (Natural History), 1969

Evans, D.H, & Loveluck, C. *Life and Economy at Early Medieval Flixborough.* Oxford, 2009

Bibliography

Evison, V.I. *Dover Buckland Anglo-Saxon Cemetery.* Historic Buildings and Monuments Commission for England, archaeological report number 6, London, 1987

- *An Anglo-Saxon Cemetery at Alton, Hampshire*, Hampshire Field Club monograph 4, Gloucester, 1988

Faussett, R.B. *Inventorium Sepulchrale; an account of some antiquities dug up at Gilton, Kingston, Sibertswold, Barfriston, Beakesbourne, Chartham and Crundale,.Kent from AD 1757 to AD 1773.* London, 1856

Fenwick, V. *Insula de Bergh excavations at Burrow Hill, Butley, Suffolk 1978-81.* Anglo-Saxon Studies in Archaeology & History 3, 1984

Fox, C. *Archaeology in the Cambridge Region,* Cambs. Univ. press, London, 1923.

Franks et al; *Molecular Psychiatry Volume 12,* 2007

Garmonsway, G.N. *Ælfric's Colloquy*, Exeter, 1991

Geake, H. *The Use of Grave-Goods in Conversion Period England, c600-850.* B.A.R. British Series, no 261, Oxford, 1997

Goodall, I. *The Iron Objects* in P. Rahtz; *The Saxon and Medieval Palaces at Cheddar, Excavations 1960-62,* BAR British Series 65, Oxford, 1979

Goodall, I.H. *Non Ferrous Metal Objects* in Rogerson,A & Dallas, C. *Excavations in Thetford, 1948-49 & 1973-80.* EAA22, 1984

- *Objects of Iron* in G. Beresford; *Goltho - The Development of an Early Medieval manor C850-1150.* English Heritage Archaeological report 4. London, 1987
- *Woodworking Tools in M. Biddle (Ed).* 1990
- *The Ironwork* in P. .Armstrong, D. Tomlinson & D.H. Evans; *Excavations at Lurk Lane Beverley, 1979-1982.* Sheffield Excavation Reprt 1, Sheffield, 1991

Goodman, W.L. *The History of Woodworking Tools,* London, 1965

Graham Cambell, J. *An Anglo-Saxon Ornamented Knife from Canterbury Kent.* Med, Arch 22, 1988

Halsall, G. *Early Medieval Cemeteries.* Skelmorlie, 1996

Hamilton, J.R.C. *Excavations at Jarlshof, Shetland.* Edinburgh, 1956

Härke, H. *Changing Symbols in a Changing Society; The Anglo-Saxon Burial Rite in the Seventh Century,* in Carver, 1992

Haslam, J. *A Middle Saxon Iron Smelting site at Ramsbury, Wilts,* in *Medieval Archaeology* vol. 24, 1980

Hawkes, S.C. & Grainger, G. *The Anglo-Saxon Cemetery at Finglesham, Kent,* Oxford University School of Archaeology Monograph 64, Oxford, 2006

Hills, C. *The Anglo-Saxon Cemetery at Spong Hill part 1.*Gressenhall, 1977

Bibliography

Hills, C. & Penn, K. *The Anglo-Saxon Cemetery at Spong Hill, North Elmham, Part II.* Report no 11, Gressenhall, 1981

Hines, J. *Anglo-Scandinavian Clasps of Classes A-C of the 3rd to 6th Centuries AD, Typology, Diffusion and Function.* Stockholm, 1993

Hinton, D.A. *A Smith in Lindsey,* The Society for Medieval Archaeology Monograph series; no 16, 2000

Hirst, S. & Clark, D. *Excavations at Mucking.* London, 1993

- *Excavations at Mucking Vo.l 3, The Anglo-Saxon Cemeteries.* Museum of London Archaeology, London, 2009

Hodges, C.C. *Anglo-Saxon Remains* in W. Page (Ed). *VCH Durham* vol 1. 1905

Inker, P. *Technology as Active Material Culture; The Quoit Brooch Style,* in *Medieval Archaeology* Vol XLIV, London 2000

Ivens, R. Bushby, P. & Shepherd, N. *Tattenhoe and Westbury; Two Deserted Medieval Settlements in Milton Keynes.* Buckinghamshire Archaeology Society Monograph series 8, 1995

James, S. & Rigby, V. *Britain and the Celtic Iron Age,* London, 1997

Kermode, P.M.C. *Knoc-y-Doonee,* Proceedingss of the Isle of Man Natural History & Antiquities Society 3, 1930

Leahy, K. *Anglo-Saxon Crafts.* Stroud, 2003

- *Interrupting the Pots- Excavation of Cleatham Anglo-Saxon Cemetery, North Lincolnshire.* C.B.A. research report 155. York, 2007

- *A Deposit of Early Medieval Iron Objects from Scraptoft, Leicestershire,* in *Medieval Archaeology* 57 (in preparation), 2013

Leary, J. *Tatberht's Lundenwic, Archaeological Excavations in Middle Saxon London,* London, 2004

Lucy, D. Tipper, J & Dickens, A. *The Anglo-Saxon Settlement and Cemetery at Bloodmoor Hill, Carlton Coleville, Suffolk.* Cambridge, 2009

MacGregor, A. *Industry and Commerce in Anglo-Scandinavian York* in R.A. Hall (ed) *Viking Age York and the North.* CBA research report 27, London, 1978

MacGregor, A. *Anglo-Saxon Finds from Lloyds Bank, Pavement and Other Sites.* The Archaeology of York, Volume 17/3, London, 1982

- *Bone, Antler, Ivory & Horn- The Technology of Skeletal Material Since the Roman Period,* London, 1985

MacGregor, A, Mainman, A.J. & Rogers, N.S.H. *Bone, Antler, Ivory and Horn from Anglo-Scandinavian & Medieval York,* CBA, The Archaeology of York vol 17- the Small finds, York, 1999

Malcolm, G. Bowsher, D. & Cowie, R. *Middle Saxon London, Excavations at the Royal Opera House 1989-99.* MoLAS Monograph 15, London, 2003

Malim, T. & Hines, J. *The Anglo-Saxon Cemetery at Edix Hill (Barrington A), Cambridgeshire.* CBA 112, York, 1998

Manning, W.H. *Catalogue of the Romano- British Iron Tools, Fittings and Weapons in the British Museum,* London, 1985

Mårtensson, A.W. (Ed) *Uppgrävt Förflutet för PK Banken I Lund,* Archaeologia Lundensia 7, 1976

Meaney, A.L. & Chadwick Hawkes, S. *Two Anglo Saxon Cemeteries at Winnall.* Soc. Med, Arch No 4, London 1970

Morris, C.A. *Early Medieval Separate Bladed Shovels from Ireland.* Royal Society of Antiquaries of Ireland III. 1981

- *A Late Saxon hoard of iron and copper-alloy artefacts from Nazeing, Essex* in *Medieval Archaeology* vol. 27, 1983
- *Craft Industry and Every Day Life; Wood and Woodworking in Anglo-Scandinavian and Medieval York.* York, 2000

Motz, L. *The Wise of the Mountain. Form, Function and Significance of the Subterranean Smith. A Study in Folklore.* Göppinger, 1983

Munksgaard, E. *A Viking Age Smith, His Tools and His Stock in Trade,* Offa 41, 1984

Nice, A. *Revue Archaeoligique de Picardie; La Necropole Merovingienne de Goudeleancourt-lès-Pierrepont (Aisne),* Numéro Special 25, 2008

Nørlund, P. *Trelleborg, Nordiske Fortidsminde 4 Part 1.* Copenhagen, 1948

O' Riordain, S.P. *Lough Gur Excavations; Carraig Aille and the Spectacles.* Proceedings of the Royal Irish Academy, 52, 1949

Ottaway, P. *Anglo-Scandinavian Ironwork from Coppergate, the Archaeology of York The Small Finds 17/6,* London, 1992

- *Lyminge, Kent. Assessment of Ironwork from the Excavations 2007-2010,* Reading, 2012
- *Products of the Blacksmith in Mid-Late Anglo-Saxon England,* published electronically at www.pjoarchaeology.co.uk, no date

Øye, I. *Textile Equipment and its Working Environment, Bryggen in Bergen C1150-1500.* The Bryggen Papers, main series Bergen, 1988

Pearson, K. Roesdahl, E. Graham-Campbell, J. & Conner, P. *The Vikings in England.* The Anglo Danish Viking Project, York, 1981

Penn, K. *Norwich Southern Bypass Part II. The Anglo-Saxon Cemetery at Harford Farm, Caister St Edmund.* EAA92, Gressenhall, 2000

Penn, K. *The Anglo-Saxon Cemetery at Shrubland Hall Quarry, Coddenham, Suffolk,* EAA report 139, Bury St Edmunds, 2011

Pollington, S. Kerr, L. & Hammond, B. *Wayland's World,* Swaffham, 2010

Bibliography

Radley, J. *Economic Aspects of Anglo-Danish York. Medieval Archaeology* 15, 1971

Richards, J.D. *The Significance of Form and Decoration of Anglo-Saxon Cremation Urns*, B.A.R. British Series 166, Oxford, 1987

Riley, D. *An Analysis of the Predominance of Left-Handed Shears in Cremation Urns from Spong Hill* (unpublished thesis), 2011

Rodgers, N.S.H. *Anglian and Other Finds from Fishergate,* Volume 17, the small finds, London, 1993

Shetelig, H. (ed) *Viking Antiquities in Great Britain and Ireland, Part II.* Oslo, 1940

Simonsen, *Smedgraven fra Ytre Elgsnes,* Viking 17, 1983

Smith, R. *An Anglo-Saxon Cemetery at Uncleby, East Riding of Yorkshire* in *Proceedings of the Society of Antiquaries*, 1912

Speake, G. *A Saxon Bed Burial on Swallowcliffe Down.* English Heritage Archaeological report 10, London, 1989

Stenton, F. (ed) *The Bayeux Tapestry,* London, 1957

Tempel, W.D. *Die Dreilagenkämme aus Hathabu Studien Zuden Kämmen der Wikingerzeit in Nord-Seeküstengebiet und Skandinavien.* Dissertation Göttingen, 1969

Theune, C. *On The Chronology of Merovingian Period Grave Goods in Alamannia* in Hines, (ed), 1999

Thomas, G. *The Late Anglo-Saxon Settlement at Bishopstone.* CBA163, York, 2010

Timby, J.R. *The Anglo-Saxon Cemetery at Empingham II, Rutland.* Oxbow Monograph 70, Oxford, 1996

Tylecote, R.F. & Gilmour, B.J.J. *The Metallography of Early Ferrous Edged Tools and Edged Weapons.* BAR 155, 1986

Ulbricht. I. *Die Geweihverarbeitung in Haithabu, Berichte über die Ausgrabungen in Haithabu 7.* Neumünster, 1978

Vince. A. (ed) *Aspects of Saxo-Norman London 2, Finds and Environmental Evidence.* London, 1991

Walton-Rogers, P. *Textile Production at 16-22 Coppergate,* Archaeology of York 17/11, CBA/YAT, York, 1997

- *Cloth and Clothing in Early Anglo-Saxon England,* York, 2007

West, S. *A Corpus of Anglo-Saxon Material from Suffolk.*EAA.84, Ipswich, 1988

Williams, P. & Newman R. *Market Lavington, Wiltshire, An Anglo-Saxon Cemetery and Settlement.* Wessex Archaeology Report 19, Salisbury, 2006.

Wheeler, R.E.M. *London and the Vikings.* London Museum Catalogue no 6. London, 1927

- *London and the Saxons,* London Museum catalogue no 6, 1935

Bibliography

Wilson, D.M. *Anglo-Saxon Carpenters Tools* in M. Claus, W. Haarnagel & K Raddatz (eds.) *Studien Zur Europäischen Vor-Und Frühgeschichte.* Neumünster, 1968

Wilson, D.M. *The Archaeology of Anglo-Saxon England,* London, 1976

Some of our other titles

Please see www.asbooks.co.uk for latest availability and website prices

First Steps in Old English
An easy to follow language course for the beginner
Stephen Pollington

A complete and easy to use Old English language course that contains all the exercises and texts needed to learn Old English. This course has been designed to be of help to a wide range of students, from those who are teaching themselves at home, to undergraduates who are learning Old English as part of their English degree course. The author has adopted a step-by-step approach that enables students of differing abilities to advance at their own pace. The course includes practice and translation exercises, a glossary of the words used in the course, and many Old English texts, including the *Battle of Brunanburh* and *Battle of Maldon*.

£16-95 272 pages

Old English Poems, Prose & Lessons   2 CDs
read by Stephen Pollington

These CDs contain lessons and texts from *First Steps in Old English*.

Tracks include: 1. Deor. 2. Beowulf – The Funeral of Scyld Scefing. 3. Engla Tocyme (The Arrival of the English). 4. Ines Domas. Two Extracts from the Laws of King Ine. 5. Deniga Hergung (The Danes' Harrying) Anglo-Saxon Chronicle Entry AD997. 6. Durham 7. The Ordeal (Be ðon ðe ordales weddigaþ) 8. Wið Dweorh (Against a Dwarf) 9. Wið Wennum (Against Wens) 10. Wið Wæteraelfadle (Against Waterelf Sickness) 11. The Nine Herbs Charm 12. Laecedomas (Leechdoms) 13. Beowulf's Greeting 14. The Battle of Brunanburh 15. A Guide to Pronunciation.
And more than 30 other lessons and extracts of Old English verse and prose.

£15 2 CDs - Free Old English transcript from www.asbooks.co.uk.

Learn Old English with Leofwin
Matt Love

This is a new approach to learning old English – as a *living language*. Leofwin and his family are your guides through six lively, entertaining, topic-based units. New vocabulary and grammar are presented in context, step by step, so that younger readers and non-language specialists can feel engaged rather than intimidated. The author has complemented the text with a wealth of illustrations. There are listening, speaking, reading and writing exercises throughout. Free soundtracks available on the Anglo-Saxon Books website.

£14.95 160 pages

Wordcraft: Concise English/Old English Dictionary and Thesaurus
Stephen Pollington

This book provides Old English equivalents to the commoner modern words in both dictionary and thesaurus formats. The Thesaurus presents vocabulary relevant to a wide range of individual topics in alphabetical lists, thus making it easily accessible to those with specific areas of interest. Each thematic listing is encoded for cross-reference from the Dictionary. The two sections will be of invaluable assistance to students of the language, as well as to those with either a general or a specific interest in the Anglo-Saxon period.

£9.95 256 pages

Anglo-Saxon Runes
John. M. Kemble

Kemble's essay *On Anglo-Saxon Runes* first appeared in the journal *Archaeologia* for 1840; it draws on the work of Wilhelm Grimm, but breaks new ground for Anglo-Saxon studies in his survey of the Ruthwell Cross and the Cynewulf poems. It is an expression both of his own indomitable spirit and of the fascination and mystery of the Runes themselves, making one of the most attractive introductions to the topic. For this edition new notes have been supplied, which include translations of Latin and Old English material quoted in the text, to make this key work in the study of runes more accessible to the general reader.

£5.95   80 pages

Looking for the Lost Gods of England
Kathleen Herbert

Kathleen Herbert sifts through the royal genealogies, charms, verse and other sources to find clues to the names and attributes of the Gods and Goddesses of the early English. The earliest account of English heathen practices reveals that they worshipped the Earth Mother and called her Nerthus. The tales, beliefs and traditions of that time are still with us in, for example, Sand able to stir our minds and imaginations.

£5.95   64 pages

Rudiments of Runelore
Stephen Pollington

This book provides both a comprehensive introduction for those coming to the subject for the first time, and a handy and inexpensive reference work for those with some knowledge of the subject. The *Abecedarium Nordmannicum* and the English, Norwegian and Icelandic rune poems are included in their original and translated form. Also included is work on the three Brandon runic inscriptions and the Norfolk 'Tiw' runes.

£5.95   88 pages

Anglo-Saxon FAQs
Stephen Pollington

125 questions and answers on a wide range of topics.

Are there any Anglo-Saxon jokes? Who was the Venerable Bede? Did the women wear make-up? What musical instruments did they have? How was food preserved? Did they have shops? Did their ships have sails? Why was Ethelred called 'Unready'? Did they have clocks? Did they celebrate Christmas? What are runes? What weapons and tactics did they use? Were there female warriors? What was the Synod of Whitby?

£9.95   128pages

Tastes of Anglo-Saxon England
Mary Savelli

These easy to follow recipes will enable you to enjoy a mix of ingredients and flavours that were widely known in Anglo-Saxon England but are rarely experienced today. In addition to the 46 recipes, there is background information about households and cooking techniques.

£5.95   80 pages

The Mead Hall The feasting tradition in Anglo-Saxon England
Stephen Pollington

This new study takes a broad look at the subject of halls and feasting in Anglo-Saxon England. The idea of the communal meal was very important among nobles and yeomen, warriors, farmers churchmen and laity. One of the aims of the book is to show that there was not just one 'feast' but two main types: the informal social occasion *gebeorscipe* and the formal, ritual gathering *symbel*.

Using the evidence of Old English texts - mainly the epic *Beowulf* and the *Anglo-Saxon Chronicles*, Stephen Pollington shows that the idea of feasting remained central to early English social traditions long after the physical reality had declined in importance.

The words of the poets and saga-writers are supported by a wealth of archaeological data dealing with halls, settlement layouts and magnificent feasting gear found in many early Anglo-Saxon graves.

Three appendices cover:
- Hall-themes in Old English verse;
- Old English and translated texts;
- The structure and origins of the warband.

£14.95   24 illustrations   296 pages

Remaking the Sutton Hoo Stone
The Ansell-Roper Replica and its Context
Paul Mortimer and Stephen Pollington

The 7th century ship burial at Sutton Hoo contains many enigmatic objects, none more so than a beautifully-worked stone with metal fittings. It is often referred to as a 'sceptre' or 'whetstone' but it may be neither.

The techniques used in making the stone and fitments display exceptional craftsmanship. So why were considerable resources devoted to creating it?

The making of a museum quality replica stone has provided new information and fresh insights which may help us answer many of the questions that have been asked about this beautiful and puzzling object.

The techniques used in making the stone are explained as is the geometry embedded within the overall design. There is also a critical review of the existing literature on the subject and a series of essays on aspects of Anglo-Saxon society that may be related to the making of the original stone.

£17.95   33 colour illustrations, 106 black & white, 196 pages

Organisations

Centingas

Centingas is a living history group devoted to the Anglo-Saxon way-of-life. The core of our membership is in the South East of England but it is constantly expanding. We have set ourselves the task of gaining expertise in the widest possible range of period crafts and skills. Our specialist areas include textiles, language and weapons.

We provide displays and information for schools and museums, and take part in re-enactment events around England.

For latest details and information visit www.centingas.co.uk

Þa Engliscan Gesiðas (The English Companions)

Þa Engliscan Gesiðas is a historical and cultural society exclusively devoted to Anglo-Saxon history. The Fellowship publishes a quarterly journal, *Wiðowinde,* and has a website with regularly updated information and discussions. Local groups arrange their own meetings and attend lectures, exhibitions and events. Members are able to share their interest with like-minded people and learn more about the origins and growth of English culture, including language, literature, archaeology, anthropology, architecture, art, religion, mythology, folklore and material culture.

For further details see www.tha-engliscan-gesithas.org.uk or write to:

Membership Secretary, The English Companions, PO Box 62790, London, SW12 2BH

Regia Anglorum

Regia Anglorum is an active group of enthusiasts who attempt to portray as accurately as possible the life and times of the people who lived in the British Isles around a thousand years ago. We investigate a wide range of crafts and have a Living History Exhibit that frequently erects some thirty tented period structures.

We have a thriving membership and 40 branches in the British Isles and United States - so there might be one near you. We especially welcome families with children.

www.regia.org   *General information* eolder@regia.org   *Membership* join@regia.org

The Sutton Hoo Society

Our aims and objectives focus on promoting research and education relating to the Anglo Saxon Royal cemetery at Sutton Hoo, Suffolk in the UK. The Society publishes a newsletter SAXON twice a year, which keeps members up to date with society activities, carries resumes of lectures and visits, and reports progress on research and publication associated with the site. If you would like to join the Society please see website: www.suttonhoo.org

Wuffing Education

Wuffing Education provides those interested in the history, archaeology, literature and culture of the Anglo-Saxons with the chance to meet experts and fellow enthusiasts for a whole day of in-depth seminars and discussions. Day Schools take place at the historic Tranmer House overlooking the burial mounds of Sutton Hoo in Suffolk.

For details of programme of events contact:-

Wuffing Education, 4 Hilly Fields, Woodbridge, Suffolk IP12 4DX

email education@wuffings.co.uk   website www.wuffings.co.uk

Tel. 01394 383908 or 01728 688749

Places to visit

Bede's World at Jarrow

Bede's world tells the remarkable story of the life and times of the Venerable Bede, 673–735 AD. Visitors can explore the origins of early medieval Northumbria and Bede's life and achievements through his own writings and the excavations of the monasteries at Jarrow and other sites.

Location – 10 miles from Newcastle upon Tyne, off the A19 near the southern entrance to the River Tyne tunnel. Bus services 526 & 527

Bede's World, Church Bank, Jarrow, Tyne and Wear, NE32 3DY

Tel. 0191 489 2106; Fax: 0191 428 2361; website: www.bedesworld.co.uk

Sutton Hoo near Woodbridge, Suffolk

Sutton Hoo is a group of low burial mounds overlooking the River Deben in south-east Suffolk. Excavations in 1939 brought to light the richest burial ever discovered in Britain – an Anglo-Saxon ship containing a magnificent treasure which has become one of the principal attractions of the British Museum. The mound from which the treasure was dug is thought to be the grave of Rædwald, an early English king who died in 624/5 AD.

This National Trust site has an excellent visitor centre, which includes a reconstruction of the burial chamber and its grave goods. Some original objects as well as replicas of the treasure are on display.

2 miles east of Woodbridge on B1083   Tel. 01394 389700

West Stow Anglo-Saxon Village

An early Anglo-Saxon Settlement reconstructed on the site where it was excavated consisting of timber and thatch hall, houses and workshop. There is also a museum containing objects found during the excavation of the site. Open all year 10am (except Christmas) Last entrance summer 4pm; winter 3-30pm. Special provision for school parties. A teachers' resource pack is available. Costumed events are held on some weekends, especially Easter Sunday and August Bank Holiday Monday. Craft courses are organised.

For further details see www.weststow.org or contact:

The Visitor Centre, West Stow Country Park, Icklingham Road, West Stow, Bury St Edmunds, Suffolk IP28 6HG   Tel. 01284 728718

Lightning Source UK Ltd.
Milton Keynes UK
UKHW051231130222
398602UK00002B/13